The Cross on Castle Rock

The Cross on Castle Rock

◆

A Childhood Memoir

George Nakagawa

iUniverse, Inc.
New York Lincoln Shanghai

The Cross on Castle Rock
A Childhood Memoir

iUniverse, Inc.

For information address:
iUniverse, Inc.
2021 Pine Lake Road, Suite 100
Lincoln, NE 68512
www.iuniverse.com

ISBN: 0-595-29613-0

Printed in the United States of America

This book is dedicated to those wise and courageous young men who never lost faith in their country and stepped forward from behind the barbed-wire fences of war relocation centers to serve in the armed forces of the United States during World War II; men like Private First Class Teruo "Ted" Fujioka, first student-body president of Heart Mountain High School, who volunteered for military service following graduation in June 1943 and made the supreme sacrifice for his country and the noble principles upon which it was founded. No finer young Americans ever graced the uniform of the United States Army.

This book is also dedicated to the equally brave young men who endured persecution and imprisonment for refusing to be drafted from the relocation centers unless their loved ones were released from confinment. This highly principled stand in defense of the Constitution of the United States and the basic human rights of Japanese Amercians was no less an act of courage.

The principle on which this country was founded and by which it has always been governed is that Americanism is a matter of mind and heart; Americanism is not, and never was, a matter of race or ancestry.

Franklin D. Roosevelt
February 1, 1943

Contents

ACKNOWLEDGEMENT

For their encouragement and assistance in this project, I am indebted to my siblings, Toshiko Katayama, Betty (Setsuko) Katayama, Fred, Giro, Sam, Kaz, and Ben. They were all most helpful in filling in the voids of my personal recollections.

Also deserving of recognition are the following individuals, who helped confirm and crystallize vague recollections:

Akira (Ken) Ikeda	Misao Shiratsuki
Tak Ikeda	Rye Tanino
Sam Inoue	Kohachi Toyota
Mitsuo (Lefty) Katayama	Mitsuye Toyota
Tak Morimoto	Frances (Tsukamaki) Tsue
Tamo Nishimura	George Yabuki
Ray Saito	Robert Yamamoto

I am also much indebted to the staffs of the Japanese American National Museum in Los Angeles and the Mayme Dear Branch of the Los Angeles Public Library for their always-cheerful assistance in accessing archival files on the Pinedale Assembly Center, the Tule Lake War Relocation Center, and the Heart Mountain War Relocation Center.

To all, many thanks. *Domo arigato*

READING JAPANESE NAMES

Most Japanese names, both given names and surnames, can be properly read by following a few simple general rules:

1. Read each vowel as a syllable.

2. Read each vowel in the following manner:
   - A is read as in "about"
   - E is read as in "egg"
   - I is read as in the second "i" in "mini"
   - O is read as in "old"
   - U is read as in "Julio"

3. Read each syllable with equal emphasis.

4. If an "N" appears in a name and is followed by another consonant, include the "N" in the syllable with the preceding vowel.

A few examples:

NAKAGAWA is read Na-ka-ga-wa

SHIRATSUKI is read Shi-ra-tsu-ki

TOSHIKO is read To-shi-ko

YOSHIO is read Yo-shi-o

GENJI is read Gen-ji

TENMA is read Ten-ma

1

BACKGROUND

On December 7, 1941, when an air attack on Pearl Harbor by Japanese naval forces propelled the United States into World War II, there were approximately 127,000 persons of Japanese ancestry residing in the continental United States. This group constituted a little less than one tenth of one percent of the American population. Roughly two-thirds were American citizens and three-fourths lived in the State of California. An additional 157,000 Japanese Americans lived in the Territory of Hawaii.

The Japanese Americans were primarily farmers and small businessmen who catered to Japanese American communities. As truck farmers, in spite of discriminatory laws that prohibited Japanese aliens from owning land, they had achieved considerable success, especially in California, where they accounted for less than two percent of the population but produced a third of all truck crops. Unfortunately, success resulting from the dedication and hard work of an ethnic minority frequently fosters not respect, but envy, fear, and discrimination.

On February 19, 1942, ten weeks after Pearl Harbor, President Franklin Delano Roosevelt signed Executive Order Number 9066, which authorized the Secretary of War to exclude from designated military areas any persons that might be considered a threat to national security. It was understood that this authority would be used by Lieutenant General John L. DeWitt, Commanding General, U.S. Army Western Defense Command and Fourth Army, to imprison, without charge or trial, approximately 120,000 persons of Japanese ancestry who were residing on the West Coast. The Executive Order was issued in spite of the fact that both the FBI and the Naval Intelligence Service, which had been closely monitoring Japanese American communities in

Hawaii and the West Coast for many years, had expressed the opinion that such drastic, constitutionally questionable action did not appear to be necessary.

In late March, soldiers began to post notices in Japanese American communities along the West Coast. These notices informed all persons of Japanese ancestry, aliens as well as "non-aliens," that they were required to report for evacuation on a date that was specified on the notice. Usually, these notices gave persons who were to be evacuated approximately five days advance notice of the evacuation.

In justifying this evacuation, General DeWitt later testified at a meeting of the Naval Affairs Subcommittee of the House of Representatives in San Francisco that:

> A Jap's a Jap…It makes no difference whether he is an American citizen or not…I don't want any of them…They are a dangerous element…There is no way to determine their loyalty.

◆   ◆   ◆

This is the story of George, a ten-year-old Nisei (second-generation Japanese American) boy who, along with this family, was evacuated from his home in Kent, Washington, on May 22, 1942. At the time, the family consisted of the parents, Mr. and Mrs. Genichi Nakagawa, and the following children:

DAUGHTERS

Toshiko, age 25

Betty (Setsuko), 13

Kiku, 8

SONS

> Itsuki (Fred), 22
>
> Giro, 21
>
> Saburo (Sam), 18
>
> Kaz, 16
>
> Harry, 14
>
> Henry (Hank), 11
>
> George, 10
>
> Ben, 6

Because there were few job opportunities for young Nisei women outside the Japanese community, Toshiko had been working as a maid for a doctor's family in Seattle. Giro had been employed on a Japanese-owned oyster farm on the coast of Washington, 120 miles away. However, both returned home a few days before evacuation in order to avoid the possibility of being sent to different camps and separated from the rest of the family. All of the other children, except Fred, who was at home resting after having been recently released from a tuberculosis sanitarium in Seattle, were students in Kent public schools.

In addition to the children above, a married daughter, Masako, age twenty-three, was living in Ibara-ichi, a small village in Hiroshima Prefecture, Japan, where both of my parents had been born and raised. I had never met Masako, because she was born in Japan and had been adopted by Uncle Kazuo, my father's youngest brother, and Aunt Shizuyo, my mother's youngest sister, who were a childless couple. Uncle Kazuo, a tall, slender man who stood a head taller than my short, stocky father, had retired in Ibara-ichi at a relatively early age after spending several years in Panama, where he had worked as a barber on a U.S. Army installation.

◆　　◆　　◆

In the spring of 1942, Kent was a small agricultural town twenty-five miles south of Seattle in the fertile White River Valley. For reasons that are not relevant to my story, the river that flowed through the valley was not the White River but the Green River. The town of Kent, including the surrounding countryside that it served, had a population of roughly 3000, of which one-quarter was of Japanese ancestry. Almost all of the Japanese families, including the Nakagawa family, made their living by growing garden vegetables such as lettuce, tomatoes, peas, and green beans on leased land.

Although the town of Kent gained notoriety as a hotbed of anti-Japanese sentiment shortly after Pearl Harbor, I was personally little affected by such sentiment prior to the evacuation. The reason for this was twofold. First, as a ten-year-old, my activities outside of school were largely restricted to within the Japanese community. I therefore had little interaction with Caucasians outside of school.

The second reason was that I was attending Kent Elementary School, where the two classes in each grade were balanced according to the first letter of the student's surname. For example, for the 1941–42 school year, all fourth-grade students whose surnames began with the letter "A" through the letter "L" were in one classroom, and all other fourth-grade students were in my class. As a result of this arrangement, students at Kent Elementary had the same classmates year after year. They therefore tended to develop a camaraderie that was not readily breached by the prejudices of adults. An equally important factor was that Mr. Frank Phipps, the principal of the school, had been born in Japan of missionary parents. He spoke the Japanese language well and had an excellent relationship with members of the local Japanese community.

THE DEPARTURE

Early in May, the army began evacuating Japanese Americans residing in the White River Valley. It started at the north end of the valley, in the town of Renton, and continued south through the tiny rural communities of Orillia and O'Brien, to the town of Kent. Each family was required to send a representative to an evacuation-control center, where he would register the family and receive instructions. Family representatives were told that family members would be allowed to bring only as many items as they could carry. This restriction caused severe problems for young parents who had small children. The family representative was also given a family number and cargo tags, upon which the family number was written in large black print. On the day of the evacuation, a tag was to be attached to each piece of cargo as well as each family member. The Nakagawa family number was 16786. Thereafter, we were to be identified not as the family of Mr. and Mrs. Genichi Nakagawa, but as family number 16786.

◆   ◆   ◆

The threat of rain was hanging heavily over the valley on the morning of Friday, May 22, 1942, when I spotted two huge army trucks lumbering slowly down the narrow gravel road that cut diagonally across the valley alongside the river. The first truck stopped at the Nakashige farm a half mile up the road. The second truck continued on to our house, which was no more than 150 feet south of the Green River.

The location of the river was vitally important to me that day because it served as the boundary between two evacuation zones. Families that lived north of the river were in the Kent zone and had been evacuated a few days earlier. Although we had always considered ourselves to be residents of Kent, we were in the Auburn zone. As a result, all of my Nisei friends, except my classmate and neighbor Kazuo Nakashige, had already left, and we were being evacuated with a bunch of strangers from the town of Auburn. Amusing as it now seems almost sixty years later, at this most critical point in my life, I was little concerned about the fact that my family and I were about to be imprisoned. I was, however, very concerned about the fact that I was not going to be making the trip to California with my friends from Kent and O'Brien.

There were two soldiers in the truck. The driver remained in the truck, a rifle clearly visible beside him. A sergeant stepped from the truck, clipboard in hand. He was wearing a round World-War-I-type helmet and leggings. Attached to his web belt was a standard forty-five-caliber army pistol. The sergeant approached the porch, where we were all waiting, and asked for the head of the family. After conferring with Fred, who had been designated as the head of the family for a few moments, the sergeant began to check names of family members off the list that was attached to his clipboard.

He then helped us load the truck and climbed into the back with us. Presumably, he was there to insure that no member of the family had a last-minute change of heart and tried to escape while en route to the Auburn Train Station.

We had been packed and ready long before the truck had pulled into our yard. A Model A Ford sedan and a half-ton Dodge pick-up had been sold for whatever we could get. Everything else that we could not carry was left unguarded in Mr. Nakatsuka's barn or was simply abandoned. There was nothing else that we could do, because we could not afford to pay for storage, and with a quarter of the population in the area leaving with only a few days advance notice, there was no market for such things as farm tools and used furniture.

◆   ◆   ◆

The train was waiting when we arrived at the Auburn train station. We were in luck. Unlike the rickety old trains that we would be riding on subsequent trips, this was a regular passenger train that had been commandeered for the trip. There was no sleeper, but the cars were clean and equipped with comfortable padded seats. More importantly, the train included a dining car. I was in hog heaven when I went for my first meal and a friendly waiter in black trousers and a neatly-pressed white coat handed me a menu and told me that I was free to choose anything that I wanted. The waiter was the first black person with whom I had ever engaged in conversation. He made a favorable impression. A man of middle age, he was friendly, personable, and helpful. For the next two days, I ordered the most expensive-looking items that were on the menu and never missed dessert.

The trip to California was quiet and uneventful. There was always at least one armed soldier in each car, but the soldiers were pleasant and conducted themselves well. Their primary mission was to prevent passengers from escaping, which was ludicrous. Why would a passenger who had willingly reported for evacuation and would now be so conspicuous outside of the train attempt to escape at a location that was not even familiar to him? Obviously, it would have made far more sense for an individual who intended to avoid imprisonment to do so before reporting for evacuation, because he would still have had a vehicle and the means to disguise himself. As it developed, the primary function of the soldiers was to regulate traffic to the dining car so as to prevent congestion and remind passengers to pull down the blinds when we passed through a town. This was not a problem, because the train was routed east through the Cascade Mountains and then south through central Washington and central Oregon, where there were very few towns.

One of the families in our car consisted of a young Issei (first-generation Japanese American) man, his attractive Nisei wife, and their three cute little daughters. The two younger girls were little more than toddlers. The soldiers generally sat in the last seat of the car and kept to themselves, but one of them played with the girls and gave them some candy. Two months later, the family, which turned out to be the Tsukamaki family, became our next door neighbors at the Tule Lake War Relocation Center. The Tsukamaki family had been living north of the Green River in the Kent zone but had their departure postponed for a week because the entire family was quarantined for a week after the girls contacted a communicable childhood illness.

PINEDALE

We arrived at the Pinedale Assembly Center on Sunday, May 24. Pinedale was located eight miles north of Fresno. It consisted of two hundred tarpaper-covered barracks arranged in eight long rows. Dispersed among these barracks were ten mess halls, twenty showers, five laundry rooms, and thirty large community outhouses. All were constructed of the cheapest available lumber. The entire eight-acre camp, which housed almost five thousand evacuees, was surrounded by a barbed-wire fence and guard towers manned by armed soldiers. Beyond the fence was a dirt road that the soldiers used when changing guard. Beyond the road were row after row of sapling fig trees. Officially, Pinedale was one of fifteen assembly centers that had been hastily prepared by the government to accommodate 120,000 persons of Japanese ancestry. By any honest definition, however, it was nothing less than a concentration camp.

A large number of friends from Kent who had arrived a few days earlier were at the main gate to greet us as we entered the camp. This was fortunate, because we were assigned to Barrack 27 in Block C, which was at the far side of the camp. Our friends turned out to be most helpful in carrying our baggage in the hot afternoon sun.

For our family of thirteen, we were given two rooms in Barrack 27. Because the choice end units, which were jokingly referred to as honeymoon suites, were reserved for families that were only being given one room, we were assigned to rooms in the middle of the barrack. In fact, families with as many as six members were being given only one room. A single electric light bulb hung down from the ceiling at the center of each room. Except for army cots, there was no other furniture. There was also virtually no privacy, because the rooms were separated only by crude partitions that did not extend to the ceiling. It was therefore possible to look into a neighbor's room by standing on a cot. At night, it was also possible to hear a baby crying at the other end of the barrack.

For many evacuees, especially the elderly and couples with small children, the summer of 1942 in Pinedale was a horror. The vast majority of evacuees were from the Pacific Northwest, where the weather, even during summer, was relatively mild. With no running water in the barrack and no electric fan, it was all but impossible to keep cool and clean in the blazing desert sun, where temperatures usually rose to over 100 degrees in the afternoon. Other problems were the smelly community outhouses, the long lines at the mess halls, the poor quality of the food, and the lack of privacy in both the barracks and the shower rooms. For many adults, idleness also became a serious problem.

Like most of the other school age children, however, I quickly adjusted to life in Pinedale. Even the outhouses were not a problem for me, because I had been using an outhouse all my life. Within days, I had made a host of new friends and began to run about the neighborhood. One of my favorite activities during my first few days in Pinedale was *oyatsu* (a mid-meal snack for children) hopping. My friends and I would get in line early so that we would be among the first to get the *oyatsu* at our own mess hall, then rush over to another mess hall for seconds. Usually, the *oyatsu* consisted of either saltine crackers or Graham crackers and milk or Kool-Aid.

For people who were fortunate enough to have been raised during the relative prosperity of post-World War II America, this may not sound like much of a treat. However, for a ten-year-old boy who had been raised during the Great Depression of the 1930s and was accustomed to school lunches consisting of stale bread and homemade wild blackberry jam through long, cold winters, this was indeed a treat. Unfortunately, after a couple of weeks, personnel who worked in the mess halls began to recognize children who did not live in their area and turn them away.

Another popular activity was playing in the shower during the middle of the hot afternoon. We were quickly forced to discontinue these showers however, when the area around the shower room began to flood due to poor drainage and a water shortage developed. One feature of the shower room is especially memorable. At the entrance to the shower was a shallow foot bath that was filled with a yellow chemical solution. This was intended to prevent the spread of athlete's foot, however, a rumor spread among the boys that the solution was actually urine. Thereafter, we all avoided putting our feet in the yellow solution by entering at the sides of the entrance and stepping on the top of the walls of the foot bath. Along with most of my friends, I continued to do this long after being convinced of the truth, because it had become a childish ritual.

Close quarters living in Pinedale presented me with one serious personal problem. At the age of ten, I still occasionally wet my bed. In Kent, this had not been a problem, because my nearest friends lived a half-mile away. I begged Mom not to air my mattress outdoors, but to no avail. Fortunately, nobody seemed to take notice, probably because there were many infants and small children in the area whose mattresses were also being aired out.

It was at Pinedale that I was first introduced to bathroom graffiti. Most of it was crude and vulgar, but some of it gave the indication of literary potential. One clever little ditty that I recall read:

> Those who write on shithouse walls,
> Should roll their shit in little balls.
> Those who read these lines of wit,
> Should eat these little balls of shit.

Almost all of the evacuees living in our neighborhood came from western Washington and were immigrant families from the area around Hiroshima, which is on the main Japanese island of Honshu. They tended to have what I thought at the time to be "common" Japanese names like Nakamura, Sato, and Yamamoto. However, one of the first boys that I befriended at Pinedale was from central California and was the son of immigrants from Okinawa, the southernmost of the forty-six Japanese prefectures. He was the first Okinawan that I had ever met and his name was Seitoku Oganeku. Although we were play-mates for only two months, the name has stuck in my mind for all these years. Imagine having a friend with a name like Gottfried Hammersmitt among a bunch of friends with names like Tom Jones and Bill Smith.

Recreational activities were quickly organized in order to keep the evacuees busy. Events included singing, dancing, wood carving, and sumo wrestling. Within a couple of weeks, there were talent shows, art exhibitions, and athletic leagues.

By far, the most popular activity at Pinedale was softball. Several categories of leagues were organized for men. There was an AA league, two A leagues, a B league and an old-timers league. There were also several leagues for young boys and girls. At Pinedale, it seemed like almost everybody except infants and old ladies were playing softball. On July 13, as the first trainloads of evacuees were leaving Pinedale for more permanent camps further inland, the Pinedale Loggers, a team comprised of young men from the White River Valley, won the AA league title and were crowned Champions of the Pinedale Assembly Center.

I played for a team that we called the Rainiers, after the Seattle Rainiers professional baseball team in the old Pacific Coast League. Not being athletically endowed, I played right field, where I was least likely to hurt the team defensively. However, because some members of the team were so small that they couldn't even hit the ball out of the infield, I batted in the middle of the line-up.

The recreation department furnished only bats and balls. Because many of the boys did not own a glove, it was customary for players coming in to bat to leave their glove on the field for members of the opposing team. In spite of this practice, there were still sometimes players in the field who did not have a glove.

One day, Tommy Yamamoto, our catcher, was hit in the back of the head with the bat as he lunged forward to catch the ball. Fortunately, the batter was small, and Tommy survived the incident with nothing more than a gash on the back of the head and a nasty headache. After that, Tommy took a lot of good-natured ribbing from teammates about being a "hard-headed Jap," which was a term that many of the Nisei jokingly used when referring to an Issei parent who was thought to be overly rigid in insisting on adhering to the customs and traditions of old Japan. Tommy and I went our separate ways after Pinedale, but after the war, we renewed our friendship in Seattle as fellow students at Highline High School.

In late June, the annoying problem of the long lines at mess halls was finally solved by issuing mess tags in ten different colors, one color for each of the mess halls. The tags were also numbered in order to indicate shifts. The problem of the long lines at the mess halls resulted from the fact that some evacuees were going to mess halls they had not been assigned to in order to eat with friends, or because they didn't like the food at their own. Still others, mostly young boys, were scoundrels who would go to a second mess hall in order to get seconds when something that they liked was being served.

On the night of Saturday, June 27, a smoker (a series of boxing matches) was held on the recreation field. My brothers Sam and Hank, who were both good boxers, participated. Sam competed in the 115-pound class and Hank in the 60-pound class. Hank's opponent was Victor Kawasaki, who was from Pacific City, a small farming community a few miles south of Kent. By agreement of the organizers, all bouts were declared draws. However, I thought that Hank was the clear winner in spite of the fact that Victor was both taller and heavier.

At the time of the smoker, Victor and Hank were total strangers, but later, in Tule Lake, the Kawasaki family moved into the same block as us, and the two boys became the best of boyhood friends.

After the war, Victor was repatriated to Japan with his family. In 1952, while stationed in the Tokyo area as an American GI, Hank visited Victor at the Kawasaki home in Hiroshima prefecture. A few years later, Victor, whose citizenship had not been revoked because he had been a minor at the time of repatriation, returned to the United States and settled in Seattle, where he established a successful travel agency.

On the third of July, my brothers Giro, Sam, and Kaz left Pinedale for Ogden, Utah, where they were to help with the sugar beet harvest. Fred was not able to accompany them because he was still recovering from his bout with tuberculosis. However, a large number of friends from the White River Valley accompanied my three brothers.

The departure of a large number of workers from the assembly centers to help with the agricultural harvest was somewhat ironic. Prior to the evacuation, the United States Government had considered a program to relocate Japanese Americans from the West Coast to agricultural states in the interior. However, the program failed because of the almost unanimous opposition of the governors of the states that would have been affected, including the governor of Utah. Now, with the evacuation not yet even completed, recruiters from some of these same states were arriving at the assembly centers in order to recruit workers to help with the harvest. The reason is that with a large number of young men leaving to enter the armed forces, a serious manpower shortage had developed on the farms.

With the closing of the Pinedale Assembly Center on the morning of Thursday, July 16, we departed on an overnight train trip to Tule Lake.

TULE LAKE

It was late afternoon the following day when we arrived at the Tule Lake War Relocation Center. The relocation center was located just south of the Oregon-California border in Modoc County, thirty-five miles southeast of Klamath Falls, Oregon.

Tule Lake was a huge complex of low tarpaper-covered buildings that spread over an area of more than a square mile. It was designed to accommodate 15,000 colonists, which was the term that was used by the *Tulean Dispatch*, the official camp newspaper, when referring to the evacuees who were incarcerated in the camp. Unlike Pinedale, the restrooms were equipped with flush toilets and rooms in the residential barracks were separated by walls that extended to the ceiling. Otherwise, it was basically the same drab cluster of tarpaper-covered barracks surrounded by barbed-wire fences and guard towers manned by armed soldiers.

The relocation center was organized into sixty-four residential blocks and seven wards. Each ward, except for Ward Six, which included an unconventional ten blocks, consisted of nine blocks. Firebreaks that were 200 feet wide separated the wards.

Each block consisted of two rows of barracks, eight barracks in each row. The first seven barracks in each row were residential. The last barrack in the first row was used as a recreation hall and the last barrack in the second row was the mess hall. Placed vertically between the two rows of barracks were two smaller buildings. The first of these two vertical buildings was a combination lavatory-shower. The other was a combination laundry room-boiler room. Except for three blocks that were used partially as schools, each block was designed to accommodate approximately 250 colonists.

Two distinctive landmarks dominated the surrounding countryside. A half-mile to the northeast of the relocation center was Rimrock, a round, treeless mountain with a top that was almost flat. Around the entire crest of the mountain was a rocky ledge that gave it the appearance of a gigantic abalone that had been partially submerged in the sand. For this reason, many of the colonists called it Abalone Mountain. My friends and I called it Horsecock Mountain.

A mile to the south of the camp was Castle Rock, another well-known landmark in the area. Like Rimrock Mountain, Castle Rock was low, wide, and treeless. It was distinctive because the east side of the mountain consisted almost entirely of a rock formation, with a vertical cliff that resembled the wall of a monstrous castle.

◆   ◆   ◆

My family was assigned to Barrack Number 4 in Block 54. The barrack, which was one hundred feet long and twenty-five feet wide, was divided into five rooms of equal size.

There were three other families in the barrack. In Room A was the Yabuki family, from Auburn, Washington. The family consisted of Mr. Yabuki, Mrs. Yabuki, son Ty, who was in his early twenties, daughter Masako, who was a high school sophomore, and my buddy Joe, who was twelve years old. Actually, his real name was George, but he was known among his friends in Block 54 as "Joe Jabuki."

In Room B was the Tsukamaki family of five that was mentioned earlier. However, after a few months, Mr. Tsukamaki became the block manager and the family moved to Barrack 7 so that Mr. Tsukamaki could be billeted in a room that was adjacent to the block manager's office.

Camp administrators appointed block managers. The primary function of the block manager was to disseminate information to residents of the block, relay concerns of residents to administrators, insure proper housekeeping within the block, and resolve minor disputes between residents. Although the block manager had little actual authority, he was most important to the welfare of residents within the block. Mr. Tsukamaki, a personable, outgoing young Issei man who was fluent in both Japanese and English, was ideally suited for the job and was much respected by both Issei and Nisei.

The Nakagawa family, now consisting of my parents and eight children between the ages of six and twenty-five, were assigned to Rooms C and D. However, after the Tsukamaki family moved to Barrack 7, we were also given Room B.

In Room E was the Itaya family, also from Auburn, Washington. The Itaya family consisted of Mr. Itaya, Mrs. Itaya, daughter Kiyoko, who was in her early twenties, and Granma Itaya, who was in her late eighties. Grandma Itaya was the oldest person that I had ever met. She had thinning gray hair, was almost toothless, and needed help to get about. Although Grandma Itaya was obviously loved and was being given the best care that was possible under the circumstances, she caused me many nightmares. I often dreamt that I had become old and helpless with nobody to love and care for me.

Mr. Itaya was an artistic handyman. At the entrance to his quarters he built an attractive Japanese rock garden. He had somehow managed to acquire cement, which he used to build a pond and stone lantern. Over a narrow part of the pond was a bridge that he had intricately carved from the trunk of a large sagebrush. Surrounding the pond was a rock garden consisting of red lava rocks and tiny sagebrush plants. Tiny white limestone pebbles bordered the entire garden. Grandma Itaya spent many hours sitting in the shade beside the garden in a wooden armchair that Mr. Itaya had fashioned from scrap lumber.

◆   ◆   ◆

Block 54 was in the northwest corner of the relocation center. Because there was no public transportation and almost all of the community facilities, such as the hospital, high school, and administrative offices, were on the south side of the relocation center, Block 54 was not considered a desirable assignment. It was, however, a very good assignment for me, because Block 54 had a large number of boys in my age group. Out of a total population of approximately two hundred and fifty, there were nineteen boys between the ages of eight and twelve living in the block. That was far more than any of the other blocks in the area.

Many of the parents in Tule Lake, as well as those in other relocation centers, soon began to express concern about the breakdown in family life and the disturbing decline in discipline among the children, especially the boys. Consideration was given to requiring that families report to the mess hall as a unit, but that idea was quickly rejected as impractical and virtually impossible to enforce. Another factor was the reluctance of camp administrators to impose further restrictions on a people who had already been imprisoned and deprived of most basic human rights.

◆   ◆   ◆

For the first few weeks, colonists other than the men and women who worked on the project farm were confined to the enclosed area of the relocation center. With school not yet in session and no organized activities for the children, there was little for us to do but hang around the block. Many of the boys were together continuously from morning to night. We ate together, played together, and showered together like members of one big family.

Marble games were the most popular pastime for the boys in Block 54 during that first summer in Tule Lake. The boys played two different games. The more popular game, which was known as the "ring game," started by drawing a circle six to eight feet in diameter in the dirt. Each player contributed two or three marbles, which were placed in the center of the circle. Two parallel lines were then drawn ten to fifteen feet apart. While standing behind one of the lines, each player would lag his shooter (a slightly oversized marble that the player would use to shoot) to the second line. The player whose shooter was closest to the second line would be rewarded with the first shot. Other players would follow in sequence.

The object of the game was to knock marbles out of the circle. If successful, the player was rewarded with a subsequent shot. This process continued until the player failed to knock a marble out of the circle. The first shot was taken from any point that the player selected, as long as it was outside the circle. If successful in knocking a marble out of the circle and the shooter was inside of the circle, the next shot was taken from the point at which the shooter had stopped. Otherwise, the next shot would be taken from a point outside of the circle.

The game could be played for "keeps" or for "funs." When played for keeps, each player kept all marbles that he had knocked out of the ring. If played for funs, marbles were counted after the game and the player who knocked the most marbles out of the ring was the winner. However, all marbles were returned to their original owners. Among the boys in Block 54, keeps was played for only a short period of time, because the more skillful players soon won all of the marbles. However, after school began, keeps was played with boys from other blocks on the school grounds.

The other marble game was called "Poison," or "Poig." For this game, a series of holes were bored into the ground. As in golf, the holes were numbered, and the object was to complete the course by putting the shooter in each hole. If a player managed to put his shooter in his next hole or hit the shooter of one of the other players, he was given an additional shot. If possible, it was therefore advantageous to knock a rival's shooter farther away from his intended hole before proceeding. After completing the course, a player became poison. Thereafter, any player whose shooter was hit by a player who had completed the course was eliminated from the game.

"Chicken fighting" was another popular pastime for the boys in Block 54. For this game, a player would put one foot behind his other leg and hold the foot with the opposite hand. With his loose hand, he would grasp his shirt in front of the chest. The object of the game was to "kill" an opponent by causing him to fall to the ground or release his grip on either the foot or the shirt. This feat was accomplished by forcefully bumping into the opponent or feigning a hit, thereby causing him to lose his balance and either fall or release his grip. Chicken fighting was usually played as a team game but was sometimes played as a free-for-all, with the last boy who was standing being the winner.

Two other popular games were "Kick the Can" and "Olly Olly Oxen Free." For Kick the Can, two teams were formed and each team drew two large circles in the ground that was out of the rival team's view. One of the circles was the team's castle and the other circle, which was in close proximity, was the prison. Some twenty-five to thirty feet away from the prison was a small circle that contained an empty can. The object of the game was to capture and imprison all members of the rival team by hitting him with a rubber ball, beanbag, or similar object while he was outside of his castle. However, all members of a team that had been imprisoned were automatically freed if a teammate managed to kick the can out of the circle before being captured himself.

Olly Olly Oxen Free began with players from two teams on opposite sides of a barrack. A player from one of the teams started the game by rolling a rubber ball over the roof while shouting "Olly Olly Oxen Free." If the ball was not caught by a player on the opposite side, it was returned with the warning, "Olly Olly Oxen Free." If the ball was caught, the player who had caught it would run, either left or right, to the opposite side of the barrack and try to hit one of the players on the rival team with the ball before that player could escape beyond the end of the barrack. If a player was hit, he was eliminated from the game. The ball was then returned to the other side of the barrack and the game continued until all of the players on one of the teams had been eliminated.

◆　　　◆　　　◆

Late in August, the Red Cross notified my parents that sister Masako had died after giving birth to her child, but that the child, a girl, was fine. A few days later, a Buddhist wake was held in our quarters. The service was attended by several family friends who had grown up with my parents in Ibara-ichi almost a half-century earlier.

After the war, we learned that Masako's husband, Masato, a private in the Imperial Japanese Army, had been killed in action almost simultaneously and that neither Masako nor Masato ever learned that their spouse had died.

Since Masako had been the only child in Uncle Kazuo's household, with their marriage, Masato had adopted the Nakagawa family name and moved into Uncle Kazuo's house. In accordance with Japanese custom, it was expected that Masato would eventually inherit the estate of Uncle Kazuo and carry on the Nakagawa family name in Ibara-ichi. With the passing of both Masako and Masato, Uncle Kazuo and Aunt Shizuyo adopted the infant child and named her Seiko. In the early 1960s, in an arrangement that had been made many years earlier, Seiko married Toshiaki, a young man from a neighboring village. Toshiaki then assumed the Nakagawa family name and moved into Uncle Kazuo's house. As this book is being written, Seiko and Toshiaki carry on the Nakagawa family name in Ibara-ichi, which is now called Ibara-mura. Their two adult children are both married and currently live in the city of Hiroshima.

◆　　　◆　　　◆

On the twenty-second of August, three boys who were playing under one of the barracks in Block 51 uncovered a skeleton. The news caused a great deal of commotion in the relocation center, until it was announced a few days later that the skeleton was that of an Indian who appeared to have been buried many years earlier.

◆   ◆   ◆

The most memorable experience during my stay in Tule Lake occurred a few weeks after my arrival. One afternoon, while playing in the men's lavatory with newfound friends, one of the boys noticed an opening in the ceiling above the commodes. It was just large enough for a small boy to pull himself into after standing on a toilet and getting a boost from friends below.

A few of us had done just that and were sitting around the opening chatting idly when we heard the sound of showers being turned on. We didn't know whether the sound was coming from the men's side of the building or the women's side, but it was quite light in the attic, so we decided to investigate. As we approached the middle of the building, we could hear the sound of young girls laughing. Because there was no partition in the attic, we simply crawled past the men's showers and peered down into the women's showers through gaps in the ceiling.

There were three teenage girls in the shower. One of the girls was the older sister of one of the boys peering down from the ceiling. We were watching the girls in embarrassed silence when one of the boys started to back away and lightly bumped into a rafter. That noise was just enough to cause one of the girls to look up and see eyes peering down from the ceiling. She screamed and rushed out of the shower room, closely followed by her companions. We also scampered out of the attic and ran from the building. That was obviously a very stupid thing to do, because if we had been seen running from the building, it would have been a simple matter to identify us as the culprits.

I was very worried and expected all hell to break loose, but strangely enough, nothing happened except that the opening in the ceiling was boarded up. I was never even asked if I had anything to do with the outrage. Evidently, the girls were so humiliated by the experience that they refused to discuss it. That was fortunate for me, because I do not believe that I would have been capable of lying in response to a direct question.

I have no idea how my parents would have reacted had it become known that one of their sons had been involved in such a scandalous affair. Like the overwhelming majority of Issei parents, they had no previous experience of this nature. Without a doubt, my three sisters would have been shamed and outraged. Except for Fred, my brothers would probably have had a hearty laugh. Fred, the disciplinarian in the family, who was very straight-laced and somewhat moralistic, would probably have had a piece of my hide.

◆   ◆   ◆

One of the other boys who participated in the shower incident was Samuel Inoue, the son of a minister in the Seventh Day Adventist Church. Aside from siblings, Sam is the only former resident of Block 54 with whom I still maintain contact almost sixty years later. To a considerable degree, our friendship was cemented over meals together in the Block 54 mess hall. Since Sam was not permitted to eat meat, which I loved, I made it a point to try to go to the mess hall with Sam and sit beside him.

The Reverend Inoue was a short, heavy-set man with a pale complexion. He was frequently seen walking about the relocation center with a somber expression, stiffly erect in a black suit. Behind Sam's back, his Block 54 buddies referred to Reverend Inoue as "The Penguin."

Years later, in 1951, with the draft board hot on our trail, Sam and I joined the Navy Reserve together in Seattle, Washington. In early 1952, we were both called to serve twenty-four months of active duty. As a result, I became the only one of eight Nakagawa boys who never served in the United States Army.

◆   ◆   ◆

Sam's best friend in Tule Lake was John Tenma, a fellow Seventh Day Adventist from Auburn, Washington, who lived in Block 49, the adjacent block to the south. John was the only boy outside of Block 54 who regularly joined us in play and mischief. Like Sam, John was a year younger than me. Unlike Sam, who was on the small side, John was a big, husky kid.

John had a mild asthmatic condition that sometimes resulted in nasal mucus running down his nose. Ordinarily, a boy with such a condition would be subjected to teasing. Although John was one of the younger boys in our group, he suffered no such indignities. Not only was he big and husky, he was also tough.

◆   ◆   ◆

In additional to the campsite, the Tule Lake War Relocation Center included almost 7,000 acres of surrounding land, much of it fertile former lake bottomland. More than 2,500 acres of this land was used by the project farm, where an almost endless variety of farm produce was grown. Like many of the able-bodied Issei men in Block 54, Dad was soon employed on the farm, where the harvest was in full swing.

For his services, Dad was paid the standard nonprofessional War Relocation Authority salary of sixteen dollars a month for a forty-four-hour workweek (less than nine cents an hour). Although nine cents an hour was slavery wages, even by standards of those times, when compared to professionals such as doctors and dentists, who were paid nineteen dollars per month, Dad was grossly overpaid. This ridiculous salary structure was the result of a political decision that had been made at the highest levels of the United States Government. In order to avoid possible charges that they were pampering people who had been imprisoned as security risks, they decided that no evacuee would be paid more than the lowest paid serviceman. In other words, an evac-uee doctor could not be paid more than a buck private, who at the time was being paid twenty-one dollars a month. In order to avoid paying a farm laborer as much as a doctor, as an expediency, all nonprofession-als were paid a standard salary of sixteen dollars a month. For a short period of time, an apprentice rate of twelve dollars a month was tried in the relocation centers. It was, however, quickly abandoned as a bureaucratic nightmare that could not possibly be justified by any potential savings to the government.

In addition to his salary, each worker was paid a clothing allowance of $3.75 for himself and each dependent over the age of sixteen, $3.25 for each dependent between the ages of eight and sixteen, and $2.25 for each dependent under the age of eight. Although the amounts that evacuees were paid was adequate to sustain a frugal lifestyle in the relo-cation center, many evacuee families suffered huge financial losses because the amounts that they earned while incarcerated was nowhere near adequate to prevent foreclosures on homes and businesses that had been left behind.

After a few weeks in Tule Lake, Fred found employment in the relo-cation center warehouse and Toshiko found work in a nursery school. Both were paid the standard salary of sixteen dollars a month.

◆   ◆   ◆

The War Relocation Authority had a daily food allowance of forty-five cents for each evacuee. For a poor, Depression-era farm boy who had looked upon such fare as bear meat, rabbit, and tempura baby trout (which I had personally poached in Smith Creek) as treats, the food at Tule Lake was generally adequate but soon became monoto-nous. At times, we seemed to practically live on pan-fried Columbia River smelts and lamb curry stew. The smelts were bony, had little taste, and were tolerable only when very hungry. At first, I loved the lamb curry stew on rice, because almost any meat was a treat. However, as time went by, the smell of curry became mildly nauseating and I began to rub as much of the curry off as I could before eating the meat and the vegetables. To this day, I partake of curry only occasionally as a concession to my wife, who loves chicken curry on rice.

◆   ◆   ◆

On the twenty-eight of August, Kaz, who had been in Ogden, Utah, working on the sugar beet harvest, rejoined the family so that he could finish his final year of high school. He was accompanied by Masami Nakashige, our former neighbor in Kent, who was also returning for his senior year of high school.

◆   ◆   ◆

Dad frequently brought fresh produce home from the project farm where he worked. Mom used them to make *tsukemono* (Japanese-style salt pickles) in the barrack and sometimes took them to the mess hall in order to supplement the mess-hall diet. Although I loved *tsukemono*, I never accompanied my parents to the mess hall. Eating with the family in the mess hall was simply not the "cool" thing to do. Instead, I ate the *tsukemono* in the barrack, as a snack. I was frequently joined by the Tsukamaki girls who lived next door. Jean and Lillian, the youngest of the three girls, who were both still preschool age, loved daikon (giant white radish) *tsukemono*, which we cut into sticks and ate like raw carrots.

◆   ◆   ◆

In early September, the restriction that limited colonists to the enclosed area of the camp was lifted. The following Sunday, a group of adults in Block 54 organized a group hike up Castle Rock for the children. From Block 54, Castle Rock looked very imposing, but we easily made it to the top and had plenty of time to enjoy the fine *bento* (Japanese-style lunch) that the mess hall crew had made for us. We then played at the top of the mountain and enjoyed the view. It was a bright fall afternoon, and we had spectacular views of the camp to the north, the lake and green project farm to the south, and majestic, snow-capped Mount Shasta, fifty miles to the southwest. Before we left Block 54, all of the hikers were called to a meeting at the mess hall. We were cautioned to be on the lookout for rattlesnakes, but not one of us saw a rattlesnake that day.

A few weeks after our hike, the congregation of one of the Christian churches in the relocation center carried railroad tiles up Castle Rock and erected a cross just west of the rock cliff that formed the east side of the mountain. On clear days, the huge whitewashed cross, which served as a source of hope and inspiration to many of the evacuees, could be clearly seen throughout the relocation center. In the fall of 1982, the original wooden cross, which had deteriorated and collapsed, was replaced with a steel cross by the California Japanese Christian Church Federation.

◆   ◆   ◆

Monday, September 14, was the first day of school in Tule Lake. There was a combination junior-senior high school on the south side of the relocation center and three elementary schools dispersed throughout the relocation center. My school, which was the largest of the three elementary schools and had two classes in each grade, was in Block 50. Since Block 50 was the adjacent block on the southwest corner of Block 54, my classroom was no more than four or five hundred feet from my barrack. This location was convenient for me because students had to return to their own mess hall for the noon meal.

My classroom occupied one third of Barrack 1 in Block 50. It was equipped with rough, unpainted stools and tables that had been rushed out of a temporary furniture factory that had been set up in one of the warehouses. It was a far cry from Miss Leach's fourth-grade classroom in the modern, newly-built Kent Elementary School, but I took no notice of my deprivation. Like any normal fifth grader on the first day of the school year, I was just eager to meet new friends and get started.

My teacher was Mrs. Hannon, a moderately overweight, auburn-haired woman in her late thirties or early forties. She was a warm, kindly lady who her pupils quickly came to love and respect. As a very undistinguished student, I never became acquainted with Mrs. Hannon on a personal basis, but my impression was that she was one of the many dedicated, highly-motivated professional educators that the War Relocation Authority had somehow managed to recruit to teach in remote, pitifully-equipped relocation center schools.

Mrs. Hannon was ably assisted by Miss Yoshie Shiratsuki, a young lady from Salinas, California, who lived in Block 46. Miss Shiratsuki was a tiny woman who stood no taller than some of the girls in the class. Under the firm, loving guidance of Mrs. Hannon and Miss Shiratsuki, our class quickly became a congenial, happy roomful of fifth graders.

One of the other students in Mrs. Hannon's class was my former neighbor, Kazuo Nakashige, who had also been in Miss Leach's class at Kent Elementary School. However, in Tule Lake, we drifted apart because we lived in different blocks and had a different circle of friends. Teruko (Terry) Sasaki and George Makiyama, the two other Nisei children who were in Miss Leach's class, lived in Block 74, which was diagonally across the relocation center from Block 54. They therefore attended a different school. I never saw either one of them while I was in Tule Lake. I did, however, occasionally see some of Terry's five older brothers when they dropped in to visit with members of my family.

Another member of Mrs. Hannon's class was my second cousin, Tom Yamasaki, who was from Penryn, California, a small agricultural community a few miles north of Sacramento. Tom's mother and my mother were first cousins and had grown up together in Japan. Tom was the biggest boy in our class. Neatly groomed with a cherubic face, he was by several years the youngest child in his family and was, in my opinion, somewhat pampered. Aside from members of my immediate family, Tom was the only close relative that I had ever met. However, although there was never a dispute between us, we never became anything more than casual friends. He simply was not my kind of guy.

One of the first orders of business at our school was to select a name for the school. In the interest of promoting a democratic atmosphere in the schools, school administrators decided to allow students in each school to participate in the name-selection process. In order to decide upon a recommendation that our class would submit to the principal's office, Mrs. Hannon requested that each student drop a handwritten ballot into a can that was circulated through the room. When the ballots were counted, the top choice was Rimrock Elementary School. In response to a couple of ballots that suggested Concentration Camp Elementary School, Mrs. Hannon assured us that the current situation was just temporary and that things would soon return to normal. Mrs. Hannon's only response to one vote for Horsecock Mountain Elementary School, which one of my friends submitted as a joke, was that "one of the ballots was not nice."

A few days later, we learned that our school had been named Rimrock Elementary School and that the other elementary schools had been named Washington Elementary School and Lincoln Elementary School. The high school was named Tri-State High School.

Our first period class after the lunch hour was music. Mrs. Hannon loved Stephen Foster, so we spent many hours singing the beautiful, romantic melodies for which Stephen Foster became so famous, songs like "Jeanie with the Light Brown Hair" and "Beautiful Dreamer."

> Beautiful dreamer, wake unto me,
> Starlight and dewdrops are waiting for thee,
> Sounds of the rude world heard in the day,
> Lulled by the moonlight have all passed away.

Beautiful dreamer, queen of my song,
List while I woo thee with soft melody,
Gone are the cares of life's busy throng,
Beautiful dreamer, awake unto me.

Beautiful dreamer, out on the sea,
Mermaids are chanting the wild Lorelei
Over the streamlet, vapors are borne,
Waiting to fade at the bright coming morn.

Beautiful dreamer, beam on my heart,
E' en as the morn on the streamlet and sea.
Then will all clouds of sorrow depart,
Beautiful dreamer, awake unto me.

Beautiful dreamer, beam on my heart
E' en as the morn on the streamlet and sea.
Then will all clouds of sorrow depart,
Beautiful dreamer, awake unto me,
Beautiful dreamer, awake unto me.

Actually, it was not considered "cool" among the fun-loving, hell-raising boys in Block 54 to sing such mushy love songs, but "cool" be damned—I too had learned to love Stephen Foster and soon found myself blasting away with apologies to nobody.

◆   ◆   ◆

It was with great anticipation that I went to the mess hall with my friends on Thanksgiving Day. I had never before had roast turkey. Because we were very poor and raised our own meat, instead of a turkey for Thanksgiving, we always made do with an old hen that had outlived her usefulness. However, I had heard so much about how good a turkey tasted that I could hardly wait. I was sorely disappointed.

In the Nakagawa family kitchen, nothing was wasted. I had grown fond of my mother's roast chicken, which I would drench with her greasy gravy. I was even fond of the neck, which was little more than a greasy piece of skin. In comparison, the roast turkey tasted dry and bland. It was not until almost fifty years later, when my cardiologist prevailed upon me to do something about an outrageously high cholesterol level, that I finally developed an appreciation for roast turkey.

◆   ◆   ◆

On January 15, 1943, the *Tulean Dispatch* reported that due to the effort of 450 volunteers, the coal crisis in Tule Lake had finally ended. The coal crisis, which had lasted for several months, stemmed from the fact that the Employment Office had been unable to recruit a sufficient number of coal handlers. A coal handler's job was a strenuous, unhealthy task that involved shoveling coal from railroad cars and delivering it to designated sites within the relocation center. Not only was the work strenuous and unhealthy, it was also very hard on clothing and shoes. Therefore, for a mere sixteen dollars a month, few colonists were willing to accept the job. Although it was never reported in the *Tulean Dispatch*, coal handlers, as well as community leaders, had tried without success to convince camp administrators that certain concessions, such as shorter work weeks and special clothing allowances, be given to coal handlers.

As a result of the shortage in coal handlers, more than one hundred railroad cars full of coal had accumulated at the railroad siding outside the relocation center. Because of the wartime shortage of railroad cars, the railroad company had threatened to place an embargo on Tule Lake, to include even the shipment of food. In order to put added pressure on residents of Tule Lake, in early December, the railroad company also withdrew fifteen railroad cars from Tule Lake that were still

full of coal. Colonists who normally worked at other jobs were therefore persuaded to "volunteer" as temporary coal handlers.

◆　　　◆　　　◆

On February 9, 1943, schools in Tule Lake were closed because the
teachers were needed to assist in the registration of all colonists seventeen years of age or older. This seemingly innocuous registration,
which was intended to serve the dual purpose of recruiting volunteers
for an all-Japanese American army combat unit and clearing other
evacuees for resettlement outside of the relocation centers, was to have
violent repercussions in all of the relocation centers and keep schools in
Tule Lake closed for more than a month. In order to understand the
reasons for this turmoil, some background knowledge is needed.

When rumors of the possible mass evacuation of Japanese Americans from the West Coast first surfaced in early 1942, the Japanese
American Citizen's League (JACL), the only national organization of
Japanese Americans, vociferously opposed the measure as both unnecessary and unconstitutional. However, in view of the overwhelming
public support for the measure and the failure of even the national
offices of the American Civil Liberties Union to speak out in opposition to this clearly unconstitutional measure, the JACL reluctantly
agreed to cooperate with the evacuation. They felt that opposition
would be futile and would undoubtedly result in bloodshed. Another
factor was that even conscientious resistance to the evacuation on constitutional grounds would be looked upon as treasonous by a general
public that was outraged by Pearl Harbor and was incapable of making
a distinction between an American of Japanese ancestry and the Japanese enemy.

Soon after Pearl Harbor, the Army began to discharge, "for the con-
venience of the Government," many of the Nisei who had been drafted
earlier. Most of the Nisei who were not discharged were reassigned to
non-sensitive housekeeping duties. In March 1942, the Selective Ser-

vice System began to classify all draft-age Nisei males as 4-F (physically not fit for duty). This was later changed to 4-C (enemy alien).

On January 28, 1943, the Secretary of War announced plans to form an army combat unit entirely of Japanese American volunteers. This announcement was followed a few days later by President Roosevelt's press release, which stated in part that, "No loyal citizen of the United States should be denied the right to exercise the responsibility of his citizenship, regardless of his ancestry."

This abrupt change in policy regarding military service for the Nisei was the result of prodding by both the War Relocation Authority and the JACL. However, the motives of the two organizations in recommending the formation of an all-Japanese American combat unit and re-instituting the draft for Nisei men were somewhat different.

War Relocation Authority officials quickly recognized the unhealthy atmosphere of the relocation centers and the impact it was having on the psyche of the evacuees. They were especially concerned about the breakdown in family life and the rapid decline in the morale and discipline of an industrious people who were guilty of nothing except their Japanese ancestry. Many War Relocation Authority officials were experienced in the administration of Indian reservations and were concerned that Japanese Americans might, like many Native Americans, become virtual wards of the government. It was therefore decided to embark on a high-priority program to quickly resettle as many evacuees as possible outside of the relocation centers. The program was hampered however, by a slow, tedious procedure for obtaining leave clearance through the FBI and a shortage of suitable situations for resettling evacuees, due in large part to skepticism on the part of the general public. After all, it was only logical to question why people who had been removed from the West Coast and incarcerated because they were not considered to be trustworthy should be considered suitable for resettlement in their neighborhoods. The War Relocation Authority believed that military service by the Nisei, especially if properly publicized, would do much to overcome this skepticism. It was also thought that military service would result in an improvement in the morale and self-esteem of the Nisei.

JACL was, however, primarily concerned about the image of the Nisei after the war if they had not served during the war, regardless of the fact that the rationale for not serving would be that they had not been allowed to serve. The reason for this seemingly paranoid concern about image was the unrelenting pressure of powerful racists, including some members of Congress, who were going so far as to advocate deporting all persons of Japanese ancestry after the war. Obviously, it would be very difficult to gain support for a proposal to deport fellow Americans who had proven themselves to be loyal Americans and had even shed their blood for the United States. News of the President's press release was therefore met with joy by pro-JACL evacuees in the relocation centers. Cynics, however, pointed out that the press release promised to restore to the Nisei only the right to die for his country.

In the tumultuous aftermath of Pearl Harbor, in spite of grave misgivings, the overwhelming majority of Japanese Americans accepted the JACL argument that evacuation had become inevitable and that it was in the best interest of the Japanese American community to cooperate in this obvious miscarriage of justice. However, following evacuation, in the idleness of imprisonment, many of the evacuees began to have second thoughts. Conditions in the assembly centers were abominable. Many evacuees were billeted in former horse stables where the stench of horse manure and urine remained. Later, conditions in the relocation centers, all of which were in remote, desolate parts of the country, were little better. In addition, evacuees had lost hundreds of millions of dollars, including crops in the fields that farmers had cultivated almost to the day of departure, because they had been given little advance notice and had also been lead to believe that failure to tend the crops would be looked upon as a deliberate attempt to sabotage the war effort.

As a result, there developed within evacuee ranks a growing sense that the good faith cooperation of the Japanese American community in the evacuation had been betrayed and that the Government was not to be trusted. In addition, growing resentment against the JACL, which had counseled cooperation in the evacuation and was now advocating that Nisei be made subject to the draft, exploded into violence against individual members of the JACL in several of the relocation centers. Why should men who had been forsaken and imprisoned by their own government now be required to shed blood for the United States while their loved ones remained imprisoned? In spite of explanations by both the JACL and army recruiters that an all-Japanese American unit would be much more effective in a campaign to enhance the image of the Nisei, many evacuees also protested that this was discriminatory. There were even suspicions among some paranoid evacuees that this recruitment was nothing less than a diabolical government plot to kill Nisei men by sending them on suicide missions. Two questions that were asked of all registrants created much controversy.

> QUESTION 27: Are you willing to serve in the armed forces of the United States on combat duty, wherever ordered?

> QUESTION 28: Will you swear unqualified allegiance to the United States of America and faithfully defend the United States from any or all attack by foreign or domestic forces, and forswear any form of allegiance or obedience to the Japanese emperor, or any other foreign government, power or organization?

Although poorly worded, Nisei male registrants in Tule Lake were informed by army recruiters that a "Yes" response to Question 27 would be interpreted as willingness to volunteer for the proposed Japanese American combat unit. Those who responded in the negative would not be classified as disloyal if they responded "Yes" to Question 28. However, registrants were informed that those responding "No" to Questions 27 and "Yes" to Question 28 might be subject to the draft at a later date. Those responding "No" to both questions were to be classified as disloyal in spite of the fact that many registrants expressed a willingness to respond "No-Yes" or even "Yes-Yes," provided that their constitutional rights were restored. Unfortunately, no such conditional responses were allowed.

For female citizens and Japanese aliens, Question 27 was an absurdity. During World War II, no American women served in combat units. Also, how could citizens of a foreign country who were not eligible for United States citizenship be asked to volunteer for military service against their own country? In their paranoia, some Issei suspected a plot by the government to kill Japanese aliens.

For the Issei, Question 27 was an absurdity that could be dispatched with a simple negative response. Question 28, however, presented a serious dilemma. Because of discriminatory immigration laws, Japanese immigrants were not eligible for United States citizenship. Therefore, if they responded "Yes" to Question 28 and foreswore allegiance to the Japanese emperor, in essence relinquishing their Japanese citizenship, they would become stateless persons. However, if they responded "No," they could be considered to be dangerous enemy aliens who could be subject to deportation after the war. Following much protest, Question 28 was changed for the Issei to read:

> Will you swear to abide by the laws of the United States and to take no action which would in any way interfere with the war effort of the United States?

Many Nisei also found Question 28 troubling because it required them to "foreswear any form of allegiance or obedience to the Japanese emperor." As native-born American citizens, no such allegiance or obedience ever existed. Was this a government ploy to induce the Nisei into admitting that at one time, such allegiance had existed? If so, would this not provide justification for the evacuation and free the government from any legal or moral obligation for having imprisoned the Nisei without charge or trial? In their confusion and frustration, a large segment of the evacuee population was beginning to attribute sinister motive to almost every instance of bureaucratic ineptitude.

Another serious shortcoming of the questionnaire for the Issei was the misleading title, "Application for Clearance." The vast majority of the Issei had suffered serious economic losses due to the evacuation. They now feared that they might be evicted from the relocation center and thrust out into an unfamiliar, possibly hostile environment where they would have no means to support themselves. Many evacuees, both Issei and Nisei, had become so paranoid and distrustful of the government that, despite assurances by the War Relocation Authority that nobody would be forced to leave Tule Lake, they refused to report for the registration.

◆   ◆   ◆

Since my sister Toshiko had relocated to Rochester, Minnesota, in early January, there were only four members of the family in Tule Lake who were required to participate in the registration. My parents completed the "Application for Clearance" form and responded "No" to Question 27 and "Yes" to the revised Question 28. They felt that they had no choice in the matter, because both Giro and Sam had tried to volunteer for military service immediately after Pearl Harbor, and my parents were well aware of the sentiments of my older siblings. Although the outcome of the war was still very much in doubt at the time of the registration, if they responded "No" to Questions 28, they thought that there was a real possibility that if the Axis Powers lost the war, they would be deported. This would, of course, result in a separation from their children.

My oldest brother, Fred, who was still convalescing from tuberculosis, completed the "Statement of United States Citizens of Japanese Ancestry" and also responded "No" to Question 27 and "Yes" to Question 28. However, he was drafted in 1945 and later served with the Army of Occupation in Germany.

Kaz was somewhat unique among the students at Tri-State High School who were required to register; although he was only seventeen years of age, he was not a citizen of the United States. Due to the Oriental Exclusion Act of 1924, no Japanese immigrants were allowed to enter the United States after that year. However, Kaz, who was born in Japan in 1925 while my mother was there caring for her sick mother, was allowed to enter the United States due to the compassion of the American consul in the city of Hiroshima. The consul made the administrative decision that since Kaz had been conceived in the United States, he could be issued a visa to enter the United States as an alien who was returning to his home.

Kaz was unique among the registrants at Tule Lake for another reason as well. His full name is Hajime Kazu Nakagawa. In Japan, it is not the custom to use a middle name. Among the Nisei, middle names are fairly common. However, either the first name or the middle name is always an English name.

This unusual situation arose because it was not anticipated, when Kaz was born, that he would be allowed to enter the United States. It was therefore expected that upon Uncle Kazuo's return from Panama, he would adopt Kaz. Kaz was therefore registered in Japan as Hajime, one of several Japanese names that identifies a first son. When he was registered in the United States, however, in order to avoid confusion, he was given the middle name Kazu and was always known among family and friends as Kaz.

Because registrants who completed the "Application for Clearance" form were not eligible to serve in the proposed Japanese American combat unit, female citizens and Japanese aliens were not briefed by army recruiters before completing the questionnaire. Therefore, not being aware that a "Yes" response to Question 27 would be interpreted as indicating a desire to volunteer for the proposed army combat unit, Kaz responded "Yes" to the question. However, his intent was to indicate only a willingness to serve in the armed forces of the United States if called upon at a later date. Since Japanese aliens were not being accepted by the armed forces, however, the misunderstanding was moot. He responded "No" to Question 28 as it was originally worded and "Yes" to the revised version. Kaz was drafted into the army in 1951 after having received his American citizenship and served in the Far East during the Korean War.

◆   ◆   ◆

During the registration, there were many heated arguments among draft-age Nisei men throughout all of the relocation centers. At one end of the spectrum were the ardent pro-JACL supporters, who believed that the future of the Nisei was in the United States and that this future could be secured only by winning over the American public with an undeniable demonstration of loyalty to the United States. These men, therefore, responded "Yes" to both Questions 27 and 28. They later gained fame as the "Go-for-Broke" men of the all-Japanese American 442nd Regimental Combat Team, the most decorated army unit of its size in World War II.

At the opposite end of the spectrum were the men who responded in the negative to Questions 27 and 28, or who refused to register, which was tantamount to responding in the negative. Most of the men who responded in the negative did so not because they were sympathetic to the cause of Japan in the war but because they had lost faith in the United States. Due to the discrimination they had encountered in the United States, especially after Pearl Harbor, they had simply become skeptical of their future in America. They were therefore unwilling to take up arms for the country of their birth. By responding in the negative, these men insured that they would not be drafted, but the decision also resulted in them being classified as disloyal by the government. As a result, many disillusioned young men who had been loyal, conscientious Americans became stigmatized as one of the infamous "No-No Boys" of World War II. Many of Fred and Kaz's closest friends in Tule Lake became stigmatized in this manner.

Included among the No-No Boys were a relatively small number of men who were actively sympathetic to Japan. Many of these were Kibei

(Americans of Japanese ancestry who were born in the United State but who had been educated in Japan), who engaged in violence against JACL leaders in several of the relocation centers and attempted to disrupt the registration.

The overwhelming majority of draft-age Nisei men who registered in the ten relocation centers responded "No" to Question 27 and "Yes" to Question 28. This included many men who had attempted to volunteer for military service prior to evacuation. Also included were a few men who had actually been drafted prior to Pearl Harbor but had been subsequently discharged because of their Japanese ancestry.

After the war, the No-No Boys were largely ostracized by the Japanese American community, which was dominated by the JACL and returning Nisei veterans. The result was an unfortunate breach in the Japanese American community that persists to this day. Fortunately, the disagreements that existed in Tule Lake between my older brothers and friends who held dissenting views resulted in no breach in friendship.

♦   ♦   ♦

My only involvement in the registration fiasco occurred on the twenty-first of February. Late in the afternoon, I was playing with my friends in the block when we heard that a large number of soldiers were assembling in the vicinity of Ward Five, which was adjacent to our own Ward Six. In spite of a warning to stay away because of possible danger, we raced towards Ward Five in order to find out what was going on.

When we first arrived in Tule Lake, there had been considerable friction between teenage boys from Ward Five, who were predominantly from the Sacramento area, and their counterparts from Ward Six, who were from Washington and Oregon. The clean-cut, light-complexioned boys from Ward Six were disdainful of the deeply-tanned Sacramento boys, who wore zoot suits and had long hair that was greased back to form a ducktail in a style that was known as a "pachuko." However, after school started and the boys became acquainted on an individual basis, the friction ceased and old animosities were quickly forgotten.

From the firebreak between the two wards, we could see a crowd gathered around Block 42. We arrived to find the block surrounded by soldiers in full battle gear, with steel helmets and fixed bayonets. They were preventing anyone from entering or leaving the block. Parked in a firebreak on the far side of the block were a large number of army trucks and staff cars.

After several minutes, young men carrying suitcases and accompanied by more soldiers began to exit the block and climb into the trucks. The obviously tense crowd, which had been conversing in muffled tones, came to life at the sight of the men. Some shouted words of encouragement to the young men, who had been defying orders to report for registration. Others began to taunt the soldiers with a passion and anger that startled and frightened me. Never before had I witnessed adults expressing such anger. It was a rude awakening for a naïve ten-year-old boy who had been only vaguely aware of the depth of the conflict that was tearing the community apart.

Because of the resistance, the registration in Tule Lake, which was originally to be completed in one week, was never completed, and the schools did not reopen until March 16, five weeks after they were closed on February 9. Although officials in Tule Lake became aware during the registration period that failure to register for clearance violated neither selective service regulations nor U.S. laws, they withheld this information from evacuees and continued to threaten them with fines and imprisonment throughout the extended registration period. This threat contributed to the chaos that followed in Tule Lake.

As was the clearance-registration drive in Tule Lake, the army-recruitment drive in the ten relocation centers for the all-Japanese American combat unit was also a dismal failure. Against a target enrollment of 3,500 men from the relocation centers, only 1,200 volunteers stepped forward. However, in Hawaii where the Japanese American population had not been incarcerated, more than 10,000 men volunteered, far exceeding the army goal. Obviously, the War Department had grossly underestimated the negative impact that the evacuation would have on the patriotism of mainland Nisei.

◆   ◆   ◆

During the registration period, there was a major snowstorm that left the ground covered with snow for several days. One day, a wild ram strayed into the relocation center in search of food. He was a beautiful animal, with fluffy white fur and majestic curled horns. For a wild animal, he did not seem to be overly afraid of human beings and allowed us to get within a couple of hundred feet of him before turning and trotting off into the surrounding hillside.

◆   ◆   ◆

Late one evening, when the snow was still on the ground, some of the boys in Block 54 got into a snowball fight with the boys from Block 53. We were all friends at Rimrock Elementary School, and it started out with a bunch of the boys playfully throwing snowballs at each other across the dirt road that separated the two blocks. However, it gradually increased in intensity, and some of the boys began to race across the road to get closer to their intended targets. Soon we were chasing the Block 53 boys, who were badly outnumbered, throughout their block. Because the snow was moist and nearly became balls of ice when packed, it hurt to get hit. The Block 53 boys, therefore, gave up the fight and went home. In triumph, we went to their lavatory and got rolls of toilet paper, which we took outside, partially unrolled and threw over the electric power lines, leaving streamers of toilet paper.

◆   ◆   ◆

A citywide marble championship started on Saturday, May 8, with playoffs in each ward. There was a Junior Division for boys aged seven, eight, and nine, and a Senior Division for ages ten, eleven and twelve. Ward Six playoffs were held in the firebreak between Ward Five and Ward Six. I competed in the Seniors Division but was quickly eliminated. However, my pal Toshio Arima, who lived in Barrack 5403 directly behind me, won the ward championship in the Junior Division. On the following Saturday, Toshio also won the citywide championship.

◆   ◆   ◆

On Saturday, May 30, the Klamath Falls Pelicans, a semi-professional team, visited the relocation center to play the Tule Lake All-Stars. I was among the huge crowd of 5,000 that witnessed the game. Compared to the Pelicans, who were all dressed in the same colorful uniforms, the Tule Lake All-Stars looked ragged, their outfits assembled from a patchwork of different uniforms. However, once the game began, the All-Stars proved to be much the better team and easily won the game by the score of 16-0. The star of the game was Tule Lake pitcher George Goto, a tall, lean sixteen-year-old junior at Tri-State High who completely dominated the Pelicans for the first five innings with his blazing fastball.

I was watching the game from along the third base line with a group of friends from Block 54. Early in the game, when the score was still close, a Pelican batter hit a looping foul ball down the third base line. Tak Ikeda, the All-Star third baseman from Tacoma, Washington, came charging after the ball and knocked me to the ground. It knocked the wind out of me, and I was gasping for breath when he helped me to my feet. It was the first time that I had ever had the wind knocked out of me, and until I caught my breath a few seconds later, I was afraid that I was going to die. Tak was wearing the purple and white jersey of the prewar Tacoma Bussei (Buddhist Youths) baseball team.

◆ ◆ ◆

It snowed on the first of June. The snowfall, which came as a complete surprise to everyone, was the latest on record in the area. It was bad news for the colonists because of the heavy damage it did to the project farm that provided most of the fresh produce for our mess halls. Especially hard hit were crops of spring greens, such as lettuce, *komatsu-na* (Japanese greens), and spinach, which farm workers were just starting to harvest.

◆ ◆ ◆

In early June, Mrs. Misao Tsukamaki, who had been our next door neighbor when we first arrived in Tule Lake, was appointed block manager, replacing her husband. Mr. Tsukamaki had left the relocation center by himself in order to find a suitable location to which he could resettle his family. Mrs. Tsukamaki's appointment was reported as noteworthy by the *Tulean Dispatch*, because she was the first woman to serve as a block manager in Tule Lake.

◆ ◆ ◆

As in Pinedale, softball was the most popular sport in Tule Lake. Almost every block had a softball team, and each ward had its own league. On Saturday, June 12, the Block 54 softball team won the Ward Six championship with a 4-2 win over Block 56. After almost a year of living together, the 250-odd residents of Block 54 had become almost like one large family. Except for infants and Issei women, almost everyone in the block attended the softball games and supported the team. Some of the Issei men in the block took up a collection and bought bright green and gold pullover jerseys for the Block 54 team, the only one in Ward Six that had any semblance of a uniform. Not only were we the best in Ward Six, we were also the flashiest.

On the following Wednesday, the Block 54 team advanced to the semifinal round of the relocation center championships with an easy 10-1 win over Block 47, the Ward Five champions. Unfortunately, two days later, Block 54 was eliminated from the championships after suffering a 4-2 loss to Block 21.

◆   ◆   ◆

Eay (pronounced "A" as in ABC) Watanabe was the star pitcher on the Block 54 team. A lean, muscular young man, Eay was a senior at Tri-State High School and a longtime friend and classmate of Kaz from their Kent public school days. Both of Eay's brothers were also members of the team. His older brother, Kay, played left field and his younger brother, Joe, was the roving shortstop. At the time, softball teams consisted of ten players. Although this tenth position was called a roving shortstop, the player in this position usually acted as a fourth outfielder who played in left field against right-handed batters and in right field against left-handed batters.

One afternoon, Eay came over for a visit to play two-handed pinochle with Kaz. The game was played with two widows. There were six cards in each widow. The high bidder was permitted to select the widow of his choice. He would then discard six cards before continuing play. With one of the widows in front of each player, Kaz was covering a portion of the six cards that were in front of him with the cards in his hand and peeking while distracting Eay with his chatter. Although it was obvious to me at the time that he was doing this as a lark, it was the first time that I had ever seen cheating in a card game.

◆　　◆　　◆

Because schools had been closed for five weeks during the registration period, summer vacation did not start in Tule Lake until after the fourth of July. The vacation began with a bit of bad news for the family. Ben's teacher had sent notice to my parents that he had been disruptive and had not been doing acceptable work in the classroom. In spite of repeated warnings from his siblings, Ben kept insisting that everything was under control. On the last day of school, we learned that Ben had flunked the second grade. In spite of considerable teasing from siblings, especially me, he seemed to take it all in stride.

◆　　◆　　◆

Despite the constant conflict and turmoil in Tule Lake, the summer of 1943 turned out to be the most fun-filled time of my life. The weather was beautiful. I was always surrounded by a large number of good friends, and we were always free to play as we pleased from morning to night, all through what turned out to be an extended summer vacation.

We frequently went swimming in an irrigation ditch located just north of the relocation center. It was illegal to swim in the ditch, because the water was stale and polluted, but we ignored the warning signs that were posted at regular intervals along the ditch. In order to avoid detection, we would hike about a mile upstream and swim in a section that had sufficient vegetation alongside the ditch to provide cover. The ditch was only a few feet wide and just barely deep enough for small boys to swim, but on hot summer afternoons, it was a godsend. Although a few of the boys owned swimming suits, we all swam "bare balls."

It was during these afternoon swimming sessions in the irrigation ditch that I first took up smoking. The smoke of choice was a Bull

Durham cigarette. Bull Durhams, which were known as "roll your own" cigarettes, were the favorite of Issei men because they were the cheapest cigarettes on the market. The tobacco was sold in a small white cotton bag with a drawstring at the top and came with a supply of thin paper sheets that were approximately the size of a business card. With a sheet of paper slightly bent around the index finger, tobacco was poured into the sheet of paper. After the tobacco had been spread evenly down the sheet of paper, the tobacco was rolled into the form of a cylinder and sealed by licking the paper along the exposed edge and pressing the exposed edge against the cylinder.

On days when none of the boys were able to sneak a bag of Bull Durham out of the house, we smoked toilet paper rolled to the size of a cigarette or "Indian tobacco," the dried broad-leafed weed that grew along the edge of the irrigation ditch. The rolled toilet paper was difficult to keep lit and gave off very little smoke. The Indian tobacco burned well and gave off plenty of smoke, but tasted terrible. It also burned the tongue. A common joke among the Block 54 boys was that the Indian tobacco, which was rolled in toilet paper, tasted as bad as a Bull Durham.

We usually went swimming in the afternoon. One evening, we decided to make a full day of it, so we stole some potatoes from the mess hall with the intention of having them for lunch the next day. The following morning, we took the potatoes to the irrigation ditch and tried to cook them in what one of the boys claimed was the Indian style. We covered the potatoes with mud and placed them in a shallow pit. We then built a fire over the top of the potatoes. It was a total failure. After spending much of the morning gathering sagebrush to keep the fire burning, the potatoes were still almost raw when we tasted them at lunchtime. Fortunately, there was still enough time to get back to the mess hall for the noon meal of lamb curry stew.

Another popular pastime during the summer was hiking. Occasionally, we climbed Castle Rock, because it was the tallest landform in the area and provided beautiful views of the surrounding countryside; but we usually chose Rimrock, because, in addition to being much closer to Block 54, there was more to do there. Along the rocky ledge of Rimrock, we played Cowboys and Indians with beanbags made from empty Bull Durham bags. We also hunted for arrowheads, rattlesnakes, and scorpions. We captured the scorpions with chopsticks that we fashioned from branches of sagebrush and placed in a one-gallon can. After capturing a sufficient number of scorpions, we would release them one at a time and burn them to death among the rocks with a magnifying glass. However, any scorpion that managed to escape under a rock before being burned to death was allowed to go free, because we had decided that it was the sportsmanlike thing to do.

◆   ◆   ◆

Power outages were a relatively common occurrence in Tule Lake. After an unusually long outage one hot summer evening, a bunch of high-school-age boys serenaded the block with one of the top hit songs of 1943.

> When the lights go on again, all over the world,
> And the boys are home again, all over the world,
> And rain or snow is all that may fall from the sky above,
> A kiss won't mean goodbye but hello to love.
>
> When the lights go on again, all over the world,
> And the ships will sail again, all over the world,
> Then we'll have time for things like wedding rings and free
>   hearts will sing,
> When the lights go on again, all over the world.

◆   ◆   ◆

On the evening of Sunday, July 11, 1943, Miss Florence Tanemura, a resident of Block 54, married Arata "Ziggy" Akahoshi, a resident of Block 25. Many weddings took place in Tule Lake, but this one was notable because Ziggy was a California boy who wore zoot suits and had a long, slick "pachuko" hairdo while Florence was a very attractive, clean-cut girl from Enumclaw, Washington. When Ziggy first began to court her in the summer of 1942, he was resented by some of the young men in the block, who considered him to be an outsider and a *yogore* (an unkempt or rowdy youth). My father and mother attended the wedding because Mr. and Mrs. Tanemura had been childhood friends of my parents in Japan.

◆   ◆   ◆

On the fifteenth of July, the War Relocation Authority announced that in response to a resolution in the United States Senate, evacuees who had been determined to be disloyal to the United States would be separated from those who had been determined to be loyal. Five days later, it was announced that Tule Lake had been designated as the relocation center to which all disloyal evacuees would be assigned, and that the loyal evacuees in Tule Lake would be transferred to one of the other nine camps. In general, disloyal evacuees were those who had refused to register, had registered but had answered Question 28 in the negative, or had previously requested repatriation to Japan. This meant that my family would soon be moving to one of the other relocation centers.

A few days later, it was reported in the heavily censored *Tulean Dispatch* that Tule Lake had been selected as the segregation center for disloyal evacuees because, as the largest of the ten relocation centers, it could be most easily expanded to accommodate more residents.

Another reason was that Tule Lake had the largest number of disloyal evacuees. In fact, although it was not reported in the *Tulean Dispatch*, forty-two percent of evacuees in Tule Lake who were seventeen years of age or older had either refused to register or responded in the negative to Question 28. The average for the nine other relocation centers was only ten percent. With a relatively homogeneous evacuee population in the ten relocation centers, why should there have been such a huge disparity? No reason was ever given by the War Relocation Authority, but topping the list of possibilities would be gross incompetence on the part of the officials who conducted the registration in Tule Lake.

The only immediate impact of the segregation announcement on me personally was that my summer vacation would be extended, because the barracks that had been utilized as classrooms during the previous school year would be needed to provide additional living quarters. It was also announced that school would not reopen in early September, as had been planned. The announcement did, however, have an impact on the games that were played by the boys in Block 54. Since almost exactly half of the boys in the block would soon be leaving Tule Lake, rather than choosing up sides for team games, as a joke, we began to match a team of Pro-Japs who would be remaining in Tule Lake against a team of Anti-Japs who would be leaving.

◆   ◆   ◆

One of the visitors to Tule Lake during the summer of 1943 was Pvt. Ryomi "Rye" Tanino, the eldest brother of my chum Matami "Mutt" Tanino. The Tanino family was from Bellevue, Washington, a small agricultural community on the eastern shore of Lake Washington. Because he had been a student at Washington State College (now Washington State University) in eastern Washington at the time of evacuation, Rye was not evacuated to Pinedale along with the rest of his family. Following completion of the 1942–43 school year, he had volunteered for military service. Like most Issei parents, especially after the evacuation, Rye's parents were not pleased to learn that their son had volunteered.

◆　　◆　　◆

There was a feeble-minded sixteen-year-old boy in Block 54. The boy was small for his age and did not attend school. He walked with a limp and talked with a slur but was generally able to care for himself. One evening in early August, he tried to rape a girl who was in her early teens. The girl was walking back to her barrack from the shower room when the feeble-minded boy grabbed her by the wrist and began to pull her towards the dry irrigation ditch that separated Blocks 56, 57, 58, and 59 from the rest of the relocation center.

I was among a group of boys who were playing in the area and noticed what was happening. We began to follow. Most of us were not immediately aware of the seriousness of the situation and were following in a playful mood when one of the older boys among us told the feeble-minded boy to let the girl go. The feeble-minded boy refused and continued to pull the girl towards the ditch. The girl struggled but seemed too scared to shout or scream. Fortunately, a young man who was in his room nearby heard the commotion and came outside to set the girl free. The rescuer then spun the feeble-minded boy around and gave him a good kick in the seat of his pants. To the best of my knowledge, that was the only punishment that the culprit received.

◆　　◆　　◆

Late in August, we were notified that we would be moving to the relocation center at Heart Mountain, Wyoming, sometime in September. Dad was not pleased, because he had requested Minidoka, Idaho, as his first choice and Heart Mountain as his second choice. However, Mom was very happy about going to Heart Mountain, in spite of the fact that the climate in Wyoming was much more sever than in Idaho.

The reason was that almost all of the former Seattle residents were in Minidoka, and Mom did not want Dad to get back together with all of his old drinking friends from Seattle.

Even in Tule Lake where Dad had only a few old drinking buddies from his bachelor days in the sawmills around Port Townsend, Dad's drinking had become a problem for Mom. From dried fruit that he managed to acquire from friends who worked in the warehouse, Dad began to make wine and invite some of his old friends over for a few drinks. Very quickly, the white sheet rock walls of the closet where he had his still became a bloody looking mess and Dad's friends were frequently drinking and carousing late into the night.

Dad's drinking sessions were not a problem for me, however, because I slept in a different room. As a matter of fact, it even had a fringe benefit. Hank and I soon learned that after a few drinks, Dad's friends had a tendency to forget to take their Bull Durham with them when they departed. We therefore learned to start checking Dad's room after each drinking session while my parents were out to breakfast. If there was more than one bag of Bull Durham on the table, we always took the bag that had the most tobacco left in it. On a couple of occasions, we took the tobacco even when there was only one bag on the table. Never were we questioned on this matter.

◆   ◆   ◆

One evening in early September, as the first trainload of loyal evacuees was about to leave Tule Lake, a farewell party was held in the mess hall for the younger children in the block. The party was organized by Evelyn Uyeda, who had just completed her sophomore year at Tri-State High School.

As we entered the mess hall, which had been decorated with crepe paper and balloons, each child was given a paper hat that Evelyn and her friends had made. After we had all been seated at tables, the party

began with the children at the tables singing, in sequence, a simple
song that Evelyn had taught us that evening.

> This is table number one, number one, number one,
> This is table number one, where is number two?

> This is table number two, number two, number two,
> This is table number two, where is number three?

> This is table number three, number three, number three,
> This is table number three, where is number four?

Early in the year 2000, while recounting my wartime camp experi-
ences at a small private party, I sang this song at my table. It was the
first time that I had sung the song since that party in Tule Lake almost
fifty-seven years earlier. Only then did I learn from somebody who was
seated at my table that the song that Evelyn had taught us was nothing
more than "Mary Had a Little Lamb" set to different lyrics.

After the opening song, we were in for a real treat—ice cream, cake,
and soda water. The party then continued with games and concluded
with "Auld Lang Syne." Although by any standards, it was a very mod-
est party, it was for me a most enjoyable and memorable affair. The
reason for this was that although I had heard a great deal about such
things as birthday parties and Christmas parties while at Kent Elementary School, I had never before attended an actual party.

A few days after the party, I went to see the Uyeda family, which
included my friends Jessie and Richard, depart for the relocation center
at Minidoka, Idaho. Approximately one year later, Betty, who had
been corresponding with Evelyn, received a telegram from Mrs. Uyeda
advising that Evelyn, as nice a young lady as I had ever met, had passed
away.

◆   ◆   ◆

On the seventeenth of September, General John L. DeWitt, who had carried out the evacuation and had later besmirched the citizenship of the Nisei by testifying to a Congressional Committee that "A Jap's a Jap" and that "you can't change him by giving him a piece of paper" was relieved of his command and transferred to a staff position in Washington, D.C. The news was received with much satisfaction in the relocation centers. General DeWitt's replacement as Commanding General, U.S. Army Western Defense Command and Fourth Army, was General Delos C. Emmons, former Army commander in Hawaii. In early 1942, General Emmons had resisted pressure to incarcerate the large Japanese American population in Hawaii and was known to have confidence in the loyalty of the Nisei.

◆   ◆   ◆

My family left Tule Lake on Thursday, September 13. A large number of family friends, including many of Fred and Kaz's friends who had either refused to register or had answered "No" to Question 28, were on hand at the railroad siding to see us off. Unlike some evacuees who were leaving Tule Lake, members of the Nakagawa family left no broken friendships behind.

Our transportation to Heart Mountain was a rickety old train that looked like it might have come straight out of an old cowboys-and-Indians movie of the 1930s. The cars were dusty. The seats were hard and the windows rattled. There was no plush dining car with uniformed waiters. Instead, the dining car, which was staffed by passengers who had been recruited for the purpose, consisted of a regular passenger car that had been converted for cafeteria-style dining, with a feeding line and crude tables and benches.

The trip to Heart Mountain was a long, circuitous three-day journey. First, we went north through the state of Oregon to the Columbia River. We then headed east along the river to Pasco, Washington, before turning north to Spokane. From Spokane, we again headed east as far as Billings, Montana, before turning southwest to Heart Mountain. At several points along the way, we were sidetracked to allow passage of trains with higher-priority cargo. A train with higher priority cargo was any train on the track that was going in the same direction.

Although the trip to Heart Mountain was a long, arduous one for the adults and small children, it was not without some good times for me. Several of my friends were on the train. Because we were now classified as loyal Americans, there were no soldiers on the train, and we were free to wander through the train visiting with each other. We played a few games of pinochle and rummy but mostly just chatted and watched the country pass by.

On the second day of the trip, while wandering through the train with friends, we came upon a young man playing his guitar. He was an acquaintance of one of the boys in our group and invited us to sing a few songs with him. Very soon, most of the young people in the car were singing along and enjoying themselves.

In one of the cars, I saw Miss Shiratsuki, my teacher at Rimrock Elementary School. She was sitting with her family. I greeted her with a nod but, being somewhat shy, did not converse with her. I never saw her after we arrived in Heart Mountain. Evidently, her family was assigned to a different part of the relocation center.

◆   ◆   ◆

During the segregation, three trains were used to transport a total of 1,339 loyal evacuees to Heart Mountain. After a brief layover at Heart Mountain, these trains returned to Tule Lake with 865 evacuees who had been classified as disloyal.

HEART MOUNTAIN

We arrived at the Heart Mountain War Relocation Center early in the afternoon of Sunday, October 3, to the blare of the renowned Heart Mountain Boy Scout Drum and Bugle Corps. After a brief welcoming speech by the project director and a very perfunctory physical examination, we were transported to our quarters. Little more than an hour after our arrival at Heart Mountain, the train departed on the return trip to Tule Lake.

Heart Mountain was built at an elevation of 4,700 feet on a vast 42,000-acre federal reclamation project in the northwestern corner of Wyoming. Sixty-five miles to the west was Yellowstone National Park. Fourteen miles to the south was the colorful town of Cody, hometown of the legendary showman and Indian scout, William F. "Buffalo Bill" Cody. An equal distance in the opposite direction on Alternate US Highway 14 was the small town of Powell.

Like Tule Lake, the countryside around Heart Mountain was characterized by prairie and low rolling hills, barren except for sparse sagebrush. The one exception was Heart Mountain, a huge rock formation eight miles to the west. Silhouetted against an expansive prairie skyline, the gigantic rock, which rose to a height of 8,123 feet above sea level, resembled the rakish smokestack of a modern ocean liner.

Originally designed to accommodate an evacuee population of 10,000, Heart Mountain was considerably smaller than Tule Lake. However, because it had several large open spaces within the area enclosed by barbed-wire fences, the relocation center gave a greater sense of spaciousness. Dominating the residential area of the camp was the high school, which had been completed only four months prior to my arrival. Built with evacuee labor on a slight mound in the center of the relocation center, the huge "E"-shaped building contained thirty-nine regular classrooms plus larger rooms for the study hall, home economics, the wood shop, and the library. In addition, there was a large combination auditorium-gymnasium that could accommodate as many as 2,000 spectators for stage events and 1,500 for basketball games. An attractive one-story building with an exterior of gray wallboard and white wooden trim, the high school was the only building in the evacuee residential area that was not covered with tarpaper. Equipped with a modern central heating system, the construction cost of this one building probably exceeded the cost of the 450 barracks in the relocation center that housed evacuees. Unfortunately, the building was to be used for only two school years.

The relocation center contained twenty residential blocks. With the exception of Block 7, which consisted of only one unit, each block contained two independent units, with each unit having a mess hall, laundry room, recreation hall, and bathroom. Therefore, in essence, a block in Heart Mountain was equivalent to two blocks in Tule Lake. In order to facilitate making a distinction between the two units in each block, the unit closest to the mountain was referred to as the "upper" unit and the other unit was called the "lower" unit.

There was one other significant difference between a residential block in Tule Lake and a residential block in Heart Mountain. In Tule Lake, each block included fourteen barracks that were used to house evacuees. These barracks, which were twenty feet wide and one hundred feet long, were arranged in two rows, with each barrack facing the back of the next barrack.

In Heart Mountain, the twelve residential barracks in each unit were twenty feet wide and one hundred and twenty feet long. However, each barrack was built to face the front of the neighboring barrack. This setup had no bearing on my relationship with friends who lived in the barrack that was in front of us, but it did have a significant bearing on my relationship with adults and small children who lived in that barrack because of the greater interaction that resulted from this arrangement.

The twenty residential blocks in Heart Mountain were not sequentially numbered. For example, the first eight blocks were numbered 1, 2, 6, 7, 8, 9, 12, and 14. Presumably, this unusual sequence resulted from the fact that the missing numbers had been assigned to plots in the original master plan that had been left as vacant lots.

My family was assigned to rooms C and D in Barrack 17 of Upper 12. Upper 12 was on the west side of the relocation center, alongside the barbed-wire fence. Beyond the fence was barren prairie that led to the base of the mountain. However, the barbed-wire fence was now largely symbolic, since evacuees were no longer restricted to the campsite. Diagonally across the relocation center were the hospital, the administrative offices, and the main gate.

Demographically, the population of Upper 12 was very different from that of Block 54. In Block 54, the typical family consisted of Issei parents and their Nisei offspring. The Issei generally ranged in age from late forties to early sixties, and their Nisei children ranged in age from approximately six to the middle twenties. Because these were farm families, they tended to be large.

In contrast, residents of Upper 12 were primarily city dwellers from Los Angeles. Like those of any other ethnic group, Japanese families from the cities were smaller than families from rural areas. As a result, although the Issei parents in Upper 12 were approximately the same age as the Issei parents in Block 54, there were very few young Nisei children in Upper 12. There were a few families in Upper 12 that consisted of Nisei parents and their Sansei (third-generation Japanese American) children, but the Sansei were usually little more than toddlers. It was therefore no coincidence that the two other large families in Upper 12, the Murata family and the Yamamoto family, each with eight children, were also former farm families from the White River Valley.

The difference in demographics had an important impact on me personally, because in the relocation centers, children within an age group tended to have a very close relationship with friends who lived in the same block and shared the same mess hall. However, in Upper 12, there was only one boy in the sixth grade with me and only one boy in the seventh grade with Hank. As a result, Hank and I frequently found ourselves playing with Ben and his friends. This is something that we had never done in Tule Lake.

My only classmate in Upper 12 was Ken Murata. Although Ken had also lived in Kent, Pinedale, and Tule Lake, I had not known him prior to Heart Mountain, because he had always lived a considerable distance away and attended different schools. By coincidence, Ken had a younger sister who was the same age as my younger sister Kiku and a younger brother who was the same age as Ben. Ken also had five older brothers who were approximately the same age as my six older brothers. Quite naturally, Ken and I quickly became best friends and constant companions.

The only boy in Upper 12 who was in the seventh grade with Hank was Tamotsu "Tamo" Nishimura, who lived next door to us in Room E with his parents, two older brothers, and an older sister. The Nishimura family was from Los Angeles and was among the original residents of Upper 12. Members of the Nishimura family were all very tall, with the oldest of the boys, Sakaye ("Sack") standing well over six feet tall. A handsome, curly-haired lad, Tamo rarely played with Hank and me but chose instead to associate primarily with high school age boys in Upper 12 who were several years older than him.

One of my favorite activities during the first few weeks in Heart Mountain was touch football in the firebreak between Upper 12 and Lower 12. The only boy in Upper 12 who owned a football was Johnny Kawasaki, a slender lad of six or seven who lived in Barrack 18. Although we considered Johnny to be a bit too small and frail to play football with us, we were forced to allow him to play in our game because he would not let us use his football unless we did. In response to his complaints about being ignored during the game, we occasionally let him carry the ball. On even rarer occasions, we threw him a pass.

Johnny, who was originally from Los Angeles, had an older sister and a younger brother who was still a toddler. Because both of his parents were Nisei, only English was spoken in the Kawasaki family, and Johnny knew only a few rudimentary phrases in the Japanese language. He was therefore my first playmate of Japanese ancestry who was not at least moderately conversant in the Japanese language.

The first order of business for me was to enroll in school, because the school year in Heart Mountain had started four weeks prior to my arrival. There were two elementary schools in the relocation center, Washington Elementary School in Block 7 and Lincoln Elementary School in Block 25. I was assigned to Washington Elementary, which was a half-mile away. Initially, this was not a problem, but I would soon learn that winters in northern Wyoming can be brutal and that I would soon find myself walking to school through howling winds and sub-zero temperatures.

The weather in the Bighorn Basin of northwestern Wyoming is generally pleasant, except for the winters, when temperatures can drop to as low as thirty degrees below zero. Because of the dry air on the prairie, during the winter, we always kept a pot of water on the potbellied heating stove in our room. Before retiring at night, we would always fill the stove with coal and the pot with water. However, we would sometimes awake the following morning to find that the fire had burned out and the small amount of water remaining in the pot had begun to freeze.

In the summertime, the temperature would occasionally rise to more than a hundred degrees Fahrenheit, but the evenings were usually cool and pleasant. Spring and fall weather was generally mild, except for occasional blasts of wintry weather that would come down from the Canadian Rockies. On the fourteenth of June, 1944, we had a severe hailstorm that lasted for more than half an hour. It caused a huge amount of loss on the project farm and even resulted in some broken windows within the relocation center. For reasons unknown, in spite of the harsh winters, the primitive facilities, and the fact that the dining and bathing facilities were separated from our living quarters, I was seldom ill while I was in Heart Mountain.

My teacher at Washington Elementary School was Mr. Ted Jennings, a tall, lanky man who appeared to be in his late thirties. Mr. Jennings could be best described as an urban cowboy. He spoke with a slight drawl and always came to school dressed in a gabardine Western-style suit with a string tie, engraved belt, cowboy boots, and a ten-gallon hat. A stern disciplinarian, Mr. Jennings tolerated neither horseplay nor indifference in the classroom. Through most of the early months of the school year, he had one foot in a cast. Any student who might be foolish enough to incur his wrath could anticipate a whack across the buttocks with one of his crutches. (None of us had yet heard of the concept of child abuse.) Although many of the students in the class wondered about what had happened to his foot, none dared ask.

Most of the students in the class disliked Mr. Jennings because he was not a friendly person and also because he was thought to be overly strict. Some of the boys even accused him of being a "Jap hater." Although anything but a teacher's pet, I tended to disagree. Certainly, I would have preferred to have Mrs. Hannon or any one of my four teachers at Kent Elementary School, but they were all women. In fairness to Mr. Jennings, I never saw him do anything more than chide a girl who was caught daydreaming, and I never saw him whack a boy who didn't deserve a good whacking. In the fall of 1941, for a few weeks prior to Pearl Harbor, I had attended a Japanese language school in Kent that met on Saturdays. My teacher was Miyazaki Sensei (Teacher), a handsome young graduate student at the University of Washington School of Engineering. In Miyazaki Sensei's class, the penalty for daydreaming or having failed to master a lesson that had been assigned the previous week was a solid rap over the head with a sawed-off broomstick. Compared to Miyazaki Sensei, Mr. Jennings seemed like a fairly reasonable fellow.

◆   ◆   ◆

A few days after our arrival in Heart Mountain, my brother Kaz, who had graduated from Tri-State High School in July, departed on a work permit to work on the potato and sugar beet harvest in Idaho. He was accompanied by several friends from Tule Lake. In early December, he returned for a short visit before departing on another work permit to work on a railroad maintenance crew in Montana. In July 1944, he returned to Heart Mountain for yet another short visit. This time, he obtained a release from the custody of the War Relocation Authority and relocated to Detroit, Michigan.

◆   ◆   ◆

One of the barracks in Upper 8, which adjoined the southwest corner of Lower 12, was used as a movie theater. It was equipped with wooden benches and an old 16mm movie projector that clicked noisily throughout a performance. Between the benches and the screen was a large open space that was used by children who preferred to squat on the floor during the performance. Admission rates were five cents for children under the age of twelve and ten cents for adults.

Movies were one of the most popular recreational outlets for evacuees in the relocation centers because admission rates were low and the latest Hollywood releases were made available. Although I had seen few movies in Tule Lake, going to the theater quickly became one of my favorite pastimes in Heart Mountain and I saw a movie almost every weekend. However, for my friends and me, the primary attraction was not the feature film but the short serial that was shown on weekends.

The serials starred comic book heroes such as Flash Gordon, the Lone Ranger, and Buck Rogers. Buck Rogers was known among the kids as "Baka" Rogers, "baka" being the Japanese word for stupid. Serial movies were shown in short installments that usually lasted four or five minutes. Each installment, except for the final one, would end with the hero or the heroine in grave danger. The youthful movie patron was thereby enticed into returning to see the next installment.

Many of the movies that were shown in Heart Mountain were war movies. In those wartime movies, the enemy, especially the Japanese, was demonized. As might be expected, youngsters in the audience jeered when the enemy appeared and cheered when he finally got his comeuppance at the end of the movie. Perhaps indicative of the evacuees' measure of self-hate, the jeers and cheers were invariably more pronounced when the object of the derisions was Japanese rather than German or Italian.

◆   ◆   ◆

On the ninth of October, I witnessed my first high school football game when I saw the Heart Mountain High Eagles play the visiting Carbon County Coyotes of Red Lodge, Montana. The smaller but faster Eagles easily won the game by the score of 25-0. Because there was little else to do on a fall afternoon, the game drew a large, enthusiastic crowd. Unfortunately, although high school football was extremely popular in Wyoming, the Eagles were able to schedule only three games during the 1943 football season. They won all three games and were never scored upon.

There were two reasons why only three games were played. Schools from nearby areas were reluctant to play at Heart Mountain because our football field did not have turf, and they were wary of playing on a hard dirt field, where the possibility of injury would be high. They were also wary of hosting the Eagles because football was a rough, contact sport. Officials of nearby schools were therefore concerned about the possibility of unruly spectators causing an ugly racial incident. The

Eagles basketball team did, however, visit neighboring high schools and compete without incident.

◆　　◆　　◆

In early November, Fred obtained employment at a cattle ranch outside of the town of Cody. He liked to refer to it as a dude ranch, but in fact, it was basically a working cattle ranch. Although Cody was only fourteen miles to the west, due to the lack of transportation, Fred lived in a bunkhouse and returned to Heart Mountain only once or twice a month. Fred's job was to groom the horses and serve as a general handyman. Unfortunately, his tenure there lasted only three months, because while feeding cattle out on the range during sub-zero weather, he contacted pneumonia and had to be hospitalized.

◆　　◆　　◆

For the vast majority of Issei women, the years spent in the relocation centers during World War II were years of leisure. With no need to cook for the family and their Nisei offspring well beyond the years when constant maternal attention was necessary, there was little that needed to be done except the laundry. For the first time in their lives, many of these women found that they had the time for such recreational activities as calligraphy, poetry, and music.

For my mother, however, there was little time for recreation and leisure because she still had a large brood to clothe, and the meager clothing allowance was not nearly adequate to prepare the family for a frigid winter in Wyoming. She therefore had a Singer sewing machine that had been stored in Mr. Nakatsuka's barn sent to us by Mr. Cappello, a former neighbor from the Panther Lake District in the hills above Kent. It was an old but attractive black console model with a mahogany cabinet, powered by a foot-operated rocker. From bolts of fabric that she would order from a Sears Roebuck catalog, she sewed bright flannel shirts and heavy corduroy trousers for Hank, Ben, and me. They were warm, durable, and usually identical. For Betty and Kiku, she sewed heavy winter dresses, skirts, and blouses. Mom never sewed anything for Harry, because Harry was too proud to wear anything that had been sewn for him by his mother.

Like most of the teenage boys in Heart Mountain, Harry usually wore a denim Levi jacket, heavy Levi trousers with a cuff four to five inches high that was made by simply folding the leg of the trouser after each washing, and a pair of engineer's boots. Engineer's boots are plain leather boots with sides that rise eight to ten inches above the heel and have a strap and buckle across the top of the foot. They were relatively expensive and were much prized by the boys in Heart Mountain. During the two years that I was in Heart Mountain, my proudest possession was a pair of black engineer's boots.

◆   ◆   ◆

Late in November, the fire department flooded the high school football field and made a huge skating rink. I was to spend many fun-filled hours on the rink, which was conveniently located between Lower 12 and the high school. On weekends, skaters brought portable radios and made small fires along the edge of the rink. My friends and I sometimes skated late into the night and had a grand time skating to the music and playing games on the ice. We scarcely noticed the sub-zero temperatures.

I was very envious of my fourteen-year-old sister, Betty, who used money that she had earned as a mess hall helper to order a beautiful pair of white figure skates from a mail-order catalog. I never owned a pair of skates while I was in Heart Mountain. Instead, I shared, with my siblings, inexpensive "clamp-on" skates that Harry had purchased at the canteen. Clamp-on skates were skates that could be adjusted to fit any length of shoe and were clamped onto the soles of ordinary street shoes.

◆   ◆   ◆

Unlike Pinedale and Tule Lake, where softball had been the most popular sport, in Heart Mountain, basketball was number one. The primary reasons for this were the severe weather in northern Wyoming, which made it impractical to play outdoor sports for much of the year, and the availability of an excellent high school gymnasium in the middle of the relocation center.

Basketball was widely played in high school intramural leagues and in community leagues for adults. These leagues ran from early fall to late spring. The high school also fielded varsity and junior varsity teams for boys that played against nearby high schools. Many of these neighboring high schools were much smaller than Heart Mountain High and were unable to field a football team. They therefore tended to place a great deal of emphasis on their basketball program, which was their only interscholastic sport. As a result of this emphasis, some of these schools were able to field teams that were very competitive, and the Heart Mountain Eagles barely managed to finish the 1943–44 basketball season with a winning record of ten wins and nine defeats.

Varsity basketball games invariably drew capacity crowds to the gymnasium. On the fourteenth of January, the Worland High School Warriors visited Heart Mountain and soundly trounced the Eagles 33-17 in front of a standing-room-only crowd. The Warriors were lead by captain Ray Saito, who visited Heart Mountain several times as the star quarterback on the football team, the star guard on the basketball team, and the star shortstop on the baseball team. Prior to World War II, the Saito family had lived in Kent, Washington, where Mr. Saito and his business partner, Mr. Hanada, operated the White River Packing Company. Dan Hanada, one of the Hanada children, had been one of the five Nisei children in my grade at Kent Elementary School. However, because children whose surname began with an "H" were always in a different classroom, Dan and I had never become anything more than casual acquaintances.

The White River Packing Company packed and shipped the produce of Japanese farmers in the valley to markets in the East and Midwest. Each summer, the company sponsored a picnic for their suppliers at a private recreational park on Puget Sound. I remembered with fondness those picnics, for which my mother always prepared a sumptuous *bento* featuring teriyaki chicken and *maki*-sushi (sushi with dried seaweed and lightly-vinegared rice wrapped around broiled eel, seasoned spinach, soy sauce fried egg, and shoe-string-sliced Japanese squash). Equally memorable for a poor, Depression-era youngster was the huge stake bed truck that was loaded with what seemed like a limitless quantity of watermelon, ice cream, and soda water.

Early in 1942, when Japanese families residing on the West Coast were being encouraged to voluntarily relocate inland in order to avoid incarceration, the Hanada family relocated to Worland. They were later joined by the Saito family, from Camp Harmony, the assembly center that had been established at what had been the site of the Western Washington State Fair in the town of Puyallup, fifteen miles south of Kent.

◆   ◆   ◆

As a result of the outstanding performance of Nisei soldiers, both at home and abroad, on January 21, 1944, Secretary of War Stimson announced that the Nisei were being returned to normal selective service status. This meant that the draft classification of all draft-age Nisei men was being changed to I-A, and that henceforth, the Nisei would be drafted for military service on the same basis as any other American citizen.

In a banner headline the following day, the *Heart Mountain Sentinel* heralded the news as an important step in returning Japanese Americans to full citizenship status. Many prominent members of the community expressed support for this change in policy, and Dillon S. Myer, the national director of the War Relocation Authority, was quoted as stating that, "The announcement by the War Department that Nisei are to be inducted into the army through the Selective Service System marks another step forward for American citizens of Japanese descent." However, there were some very serious problems on the horizon.

Many of the evacuees in the relocation centers were deeply troubled by continuing discrimination against the Nisei. Why should the Nisei be limited to serving in an army that would probably assign them to a segregated combat unit that, from all indications, was being given the most hazardous assignments? Why was the government continuing to prohibit Nisei from serving in the Navy, the Marines, and the Coast Guard? Even more troubling was the incongruity of drafting men from the confines of a desolate detention camp, where their loved ones would continue to be confined. After all, it was one thing for the War Department to solicit volunteers from the relocation centers, but to draft men under such circumstances was more than many of the evacuees were prepared to accept. As a result, various forms of resistance to the draft surfaced in all of the relocation centers. However, Heart Mountain was the only relocation center in which significant organized resistance to the draft developed.

The resistance began with a group of men who organized themselves into what became known as the Heart Mountain Fair Play Committee. The primary objective of the Fair Play Committee, which eventually attracted almost 300 dues-paying members, was to test the legality of drafting men from the relocation centers and to organize resistance to the draft until the civil rights of the Nisei had been fully restored. Accordingly, the committee encouraged men in Heart Mountain to refuse to report for their pre-induction physical examination. The committee also obtained the services of a prominent Caucasian attorney in Denver. In response, federal authorities banished leaders of the

Fair Play Committee to Tule Lake and ordered the arrest of any Nisei who failed to report for the draft.

◆   ◆   ◆

On the twenty-fourth of April, Technical Sergeant Ben Kuroki, the first Nisei war hero of World War II, arrived in Heart Mountain to begin a tour of three relocation centers. Sergeant Kuroki was a twenty-five-year-old Nisei who had been born and raised on his family farm in western Nebraska. Shortly after Pearl Harbor, Kuroki had volunteered for military service and somehow managed to gain acceptance into the Army Air Corps, an extraordinary feat at a time when many Nisei men were being discharged from the army.

As a tail gunner on a B-24 Liberator, Kuroki participated in some of the most hazardous bombing missions of World War II, including the famous August 1943 raid on the Romanian oil fields at Ploesti, which was launched from desert bases in North Africa. At a time when twenty-five combat missions qualified an aviator to rotate back to the United States, Kuroki had voluntarily completed five additional missions and returned to the United States a much-decorated war hero. Following highly favorable national publicity, including a story in *Time* magazine, the War Department decided to send him on public-relations visits to relocation centers in order to improve morale and promote patriotism in the camps.

During his six-day stay in Heart Mountain, Sergeant Kuroki was honored at a host of testimonial gatherings, where he was lionized as an American hero and a role model for the Nisei. He also met with virtually every segment of the population in Heart Mountain, including members and supporters of the Fair Play Committee. At the time of his meeting with members of the Fair Play Committee, many members had already been jailed for failing to report for the draft.

The meeting was heated and acrimonious. Members of the Fair Play Committee chastised the sergeant for being an ignorant, flag-waving dupe for a racist government. They also accused him of having absolutely no understanding of the true nature of their grievance. The sergeant responded in kind by ridiculing members of the Fair Play Committee for having any illusions about the inevitable defeat of Imperial Japan. Obviously, in such an acrimonious atmosphere, not even the slightest convergence of views was possible, and the meeting turned out to be a complete waste of time for all parties.

As part of his tour of Heart Mountain, Sergeant Kuroki visited the two elementary schools as well as the high school. At my school, the sergeant addressed the student body at an outdoor gathering, for which a small portable stage had been erected between the two rows of barracks. Although a slightly built man of little more than average height for a Nisei, the sergeant was an impressive figure in his neatly-pressed uniform adorned with colorful ribbons. After a stirring speech in which the sergeant extolled the virtues of democracy and expressed confidence in a better and more just America after the war, he signed autographs for a swarm of adoring young fans. Later that day, the sergeant was greeted by equally enthusiastic students at the other two schools.

◆   ◆   ◆

In early May, a federal grand jury in Cheyenne indicted sixty-three members of the Fair Play Committee on charges of violating the Selective Services Act. On June 26, following a non-jury trial that lasted one week, Federal Judge T. Blake Kennedy found all sixty-three men guilty as charged and sentenced them to three years in a federal penitentiary.

Shortly after that trial, the federal government also brought to trial seven officers of the Fair Play Committee, as well as James Omura, English editor of the *Rocky Mountain Shimpo*, a small bilingual newspaper in Denver. Mr. Omura was the only editor in the country who had given the Fair Play Committee editorial support.

Mr. Omura was acquitted on freedom of the press grounds, but the seven others were found guilty and were also imprisoned. A few months later, however, Mr. A. L. Wirin, the lawyer from the American Civil Liberties Union who had originally defended the seven men, was able to have the guilty verdicts overturned on appeal and the seven men were released.

◆   ◆   ◆

As a result of the drafting of young men from the relocation centers and the intensified effort of the War Relocation Authority to resettle evacuees outside of the camps, the population in the relocation centers began to decline significantly in the first half of 1944. The decision was therefore made to close the relocation centers at Jerome, Arkansas, and reassign the remaining residents to the other relocation centers. On the fifteenth of June, 500 former residents of Jerome, the last relocation center to open and the first to close, arrived in Heart Mountain. Unfortunately, I found no new friends among the former Jerome residents who moved into Upper 12.

◆   ◆   ◆

In contrast to the two previous summers, the summer of 1944 was quiet and uneventful. Because there were so few boys in Upper 12 that it was difficult to organize team games, there was little to do except loaf around the barracks or go to the swimming pool. The swimming pool was located in the southeast corner of the relocation center a few hundred yards beyond Block 7, where I had attended school. More of a miniature lake than a swimming pool, it had been created by diverting an irrigation ditch into a small ravine at the edge of a twenty-six-acre field that was being cultivated as part of the thousand-acre project farm. The field was the only portion of the project farm that was located within the enclosed area of the relocation center. Although somewhat primitive, the pool was an important recreational facility and a popular gathering place during the short, hot summer. This was the place where the youth of Heart Mountain went not just to swim and cool off but to see and be seen.

From my perspective, however, the pool had some serious short-comings when compared to the filthy irrigation ditch in Tule Lake where I had spent much of the previous summer. During operating hours, lifeguards managed the facility. Horseplay, especially in the pool and around the diving platform, was strictly prohibited. Also prohibited was smoking by obviously underage children. There was therefore little to do except swim, sunbathe, or girl-watch, which was an interest that I had just begun to cultivate.

◆   ◆   ◆

On a few occasions during the summer, my friends and I went hiking to the Shoshone River. The river ran parallel to US Alternate Highway 14A, a mile to the east of the main gate. It was very shallow during the summer, so we could easily wade across and hike into the hills on the opposite side. The river was lined with trees and bushes, but they could not be seen from the relocation center because the river was in a deep ravine.

One day, as we reached the bluff above the river, we saw a small herd of wild mustangs watering in the river a mile or so to the south. They were beautiful. A couple of the mustangs were black, but most were varying shades of brown. We tried to sneak up on them in order to get a better look, but got no more than two or three hundred feet closer before they suddenly bolted off into the rolling hills on the opposite side of the river.

◆   ◆   ◆

A few hundred feet west of Upper 12, within the enclosed area of the relocation center, was the Heart Mountain Victory Garden. The Victory Garden was a five-and-a-half-acre plot of land that had been set aside so that any evacuee who might be so inclined could obtain a parcel of land for the purpose of growing vegetables for personal use. Seeds were sold at the canteen and fertilizer was available free of charge at either the project chicken farm or the hog farm. Although an experienced farmer, my dad did not avail himself of this opportunity because he had a job on the project vegetable farm and had access to an ample supply of fresh vegetables during the growing season.

My friends and I sometimes wandered through the Victory Garden, because it was the only place on the west side of the relocation center that had a significant amount of greenery. The garden was an oasis in the middle of a barren prairie. There seemed to be competition among the growers, mostly elderly Issei men and women, to see who could cultivate the most attractive plot. Most of the plots were meticulously maintained, with nary a weed to be seen. Obviously, a great deal of attention was being devoted to these plots by the old men and women, who probably had little else to do in the relocation center.

I was amazed to see what could be grown on a barren prairie with the proper combination of water, fertilizer, and expertise. There were lush, green vegetables, beautiful flowers, and even some cantaloupes and watermelons. Most of the cantaloupes and watermelons were, however, somewhat small.

One bright moonlit night, I was sitting on the steps to our quarters chatting idly with Hank and Ken Murata when the conversation turned to food. Someone suggested that we go out to the Victory Garden and steal an especially big cantaloupe that we had seen that afternoon. In the bright moonlight, we had no difficulty finding the cantaloupe that we had in mind. We dared not bring it back to the camp, so we cut it open on the spot with Ken's pocketknife and began to eat. Although it looked ripe and juicy when we had seen it earlier in the day, it was hard, tasteless, and obviously not yet ripe. We threw it away and returned to the camp. In order to avoid being seen entering Upper 12 from the direction of the Victory Garden, we entered the camp from Upper 9, which was adjacent to Upper 12.

That night, as I lay on my cot waiting for sleep to come, I was troubled by a guilty conscience. It was one thing to engage in petty mischief, but stealing was different. That cantaloupe might have been somebody's pride and joy. Perhaps it belonged to some lonely old man who had nothing else that he could shower with his love and attention. I made up my mind that never again would I participate in such a stupid, mean-spirited act.

◆　　　◆　　　◆

What turned out to be the final year of school at Heart Mountain High School began on Monday, September 4, 1944. Although commonly referred to as a high school, Heart Mountain High was actually a combination of a junior high school that served students in grades seven and eight, and a senior high school that served students in grades nine through twelve. In the junior high school, students were given a standardized schedule of classes that applied to all students in that grade. In the high school, class schedules were tailored to suit the interests of the individual student. Reflecting the unusual demographics of Heart Mountain's population, the upper grades of the school were much larger than the lower grades. For example, although the graduating class of 1944 at Heart Mountain High had numbered more than 300, there was barely half that number in the seventh grade, in spite of the influx of a few students from the Jerome Relocation Center in June.

Students in the seventh and eighth grades were assigned to their homeroom according to their academic record for the previous year.

Accordingly, seventh graders with the best grades for the previous year were assigned to Homeroom 7-1 and students with the poorest grades were assigned to Homeroom 7-4. In order to create some semblance of gender balance, however, liberties were taken in moving some of the boys up to a higher level and some of the girls to a lower level. Homeroom assignments were very important to the students in the seventh and eighth grades, because, unlike in the higher grades, these students would be with the same classmates throughout the day. In other words, all students in the homeroom went from one classroom to the next classroom as a group.

On the first day of school, I found my name on the list for Homeroom 7-3. My initial reaction was one of disappointment, because I had been hoping to be assigned to 7-4, where I expected that most of my friends would be assigned. Upon reflection, however, I came to the conclusion that 7-3 was an excellent compromise. I certainly didn't want to be in 7-1 with all of the girls and the "goody-goody" boys. On the other hand, neither did I really want to be in 7-4, because my brother Hank had been in 7-4 the previous year and was now in 8-4. I certainly didn't want family and friends to think that I was just another dummy, like Hank! After coming to his senses as a GI in Japan and Korea during the Korean War, the dummy Hank went on to graduate from the University of Washington with a degree in mechanical engineering.

Two of my teachers were married and had spouses who also taught at Heart Mountain High. Mr. Clifford Cowger, a personable, youthful-looking man, was my mathematics teacher. His wife, Phyllis, was a music teacher in the high school. The Cowgers were very popular figures at Heart Mountain High because Mr. Cowger used his automobile to provide transportation for the high school basketball team when the team visited neighboring schools. Also, Mrs. Cowger, a dark-haired, attractive woman, conducted both the high school band and orchestra.

My favorite teacher at Heart Mountain High was my music teacher, Mrs. Mona Rudolph. Like my mother, Mrs. Rudolph was a gentle, infinitely patient woman. Also like my mother, who never raised a hand to me in anger, Mrs. Rudolph was inclined to discipline a wayward child by appealing to the child's better nature. She was not, however, a pushover. Although by nature a gentle person, she was also an experienced teacher. If necessary, she would not hesitate to dress down a chronically disruptive student in order to maintain order in the class.

One day, Mrs. Rudolph turned from writing musical notes on the blackboard and caught me throwing a wad of paper at one of the other boys in the back of the room. This action on my part was in response to a friend at the back of the room who had hit me in the back of the head with that same wad of paper. Although Mrs. Rudolph had previously caught me engaging in such horseplay, she only gently rebuked me. After the class, however, she asked me to stay behind for a minute. Since music was the last class before the lunch break, there was plenty of time.

Mrs. Rudolph began by telling me that I was a good singer and that she knew that I was a good boy. She then told me that she would be very appreciative if I would cooperate with her by not causing disturbances in the classroom. I apologized and left for the Upper 12 mess hall, embarrassed and mildly amused. Mrs. Rudolph had no further problems with me in her classroom, but to this day, I remain incapable of carrying any tune other than the simplest nursery school melody.

Mrs. Rudolph's husband, Talbot, taught physical education and vocational education classes in the high school. He also served as coach of the junior varsity football and basketball teams. The Rudolphs' son, Bob, a sophomore at Heart Mountain High, was a member of the junior varsity football team. The Rudolphs also had a daughter, Shirley, who was one of the top scholars among the eighth graders.

There were two other Caucasian boys at Heart Mountain High, the Kirby twins, who were in Homeroom 7-1. The twins were handsome kids, blond and of average size for seventh-grade boys in the school. Many of the girls in 7-3 said that the twins were cute.

It was during the first few days of the school year that I fell in love for the first time. Her name was Aiko and she was a classmate in 7-3. Aiko was a pretty, gracefully, slender little girl and was somewhat darker than most of the other girls in the class, presumably from having spent a lot of time out in the sun over the summer. Although she had also attended Washington Elementary School during the previous year, she had not been in Mr. Jennings' class, and I had not noticed her until the start of the current school year. Quite typically for a group of young Nisei kids, the students in 7-3 tended to be very shy towards members of the opposite sex. There was therefore little interaction between the boys and the girls in the class.

I was madly in love with Aiko and kept stealing glances at her in the classroom. I was also losing sleep over her. Unfortunately, Aiko seemed oblivious to the fact that she and I were on the same planet. I dared not ask one of my buddies to approach her on my behalf for fear of being teased and was much too shy to approach her personally. Thus did end my first short-lived taste of unrequited love.

◆　　　◆　　　◆

On the fourth of September, the same day that school began, Giro arrived in Heart Mountain for a short visit. He had returned home to visit the family because he had recently passed his pre-induction physical examination and was about to enter the Army. Giro was my favorite older brother. Not only was he an affable young man who had been a member of the championship Kent High School football team in the fall of 1938, he was also the only one of my older brothers who always seemed to have some money in his pocket. I knew that I could count on him for a small monetary gift, and in those days, even a nickel was good for a movie or an ice cream cone at the canteen.

On the first Saturday after his arrival in Heart Mountain, Giro took Hank, Kiku, Ben, and me on a one-day outing to the town of Powell. It was a very exciting day for me, because, except for the train rides to Pinedale, Tule Lake, and Heart Mountain, I had not been on the "outside" for two and a half years. Actually, I would have preferred to go to Cody, since it was the famous hometown of "Buffalo Bill" Cody and Powell was just another hick town. However, Giro wanted nothing to do with Cody. Cody had a reputation for having a large anti-Japanese element, whereas Powell was known to be relatively hospitable to visitors from Heart Mountain. As a result, Giro insisted that he was not going to be leaving any of his money in Cody. Another consideration was the fact that some business establishments in Cody had "No Japs Wanted" signs in their windows, and Giro did not want to subject young siblings to such indignities.

It was a long mile-and-a-half walk through the entire relocation center, past the hospital and the military police compound, to the main gate, where we were to board the bus to Powell. Because it was a warm, sunny afternoon, the sentry on duty at the gate was standing outside the sentry box in the shade and did not notice us approaching until we were only a few feet away. He looked very young and appeared to be a bit embarrassed as Giro handed him our passes. After a fleeting glance at the passes, the sentry waved us through the gate. A few minutes later, a Nisei soldier, a corporal who was accompanied by a young lady, rushed up to the gate just as the bus arrived. Without a word, the sentry waved them through the gate.

The bus was empty except for two gray-haired ladies who were sitting together in the back of the bus and an old cowboy who was sitting in the front of the bus talking to the driver. They took no notice of us as we entered the bus. The cowboy was wearing a sweat-stained tengallon hat. He looked and smelled like he had just come in from a long, dusty cattle drive. One of the ladies smiled and winked at us through her round, steel-rimmed glasses as the seven of us joined the old ladies in the back of the bus.

With a population of roughly 2000, Powell was a typical small American town. The business district consisted of a movie theater, two gas stations, and a couple of dozen other small business establishments along US Alternate Highway 14A that ran from Yellowstone National Park, through Cody and Powell, to the junction of State Highway 114 at Garland, five miles to the northeast.

The first thing that we wanted to do in Powell was find a soda fountain where we could get milkshakes, because milkshakes were not available in Heart Mountain. Except for Giro, none of us had ever had a milkshake. We all longed for a milkshake because Harry had whet our appetite by constantly reminiscing about the delicious ones that he had enjoyed before the war at the Kent Drug Store, with his old Panther Lake Elementary School pal, Donald Kalb.

Just as we had hoped, there was a drug store in Powell that had a soda fountain. We ordered different flavors so that we could exchange sips. The chocolate and vanilla shakes were delicious, but I thought that the strawberry milk shake that I ordered was the most delicious thing that I had ever tasted.

As we were leaving the drug store, someone noticed that the matinee was about to begin at the movie theater across the street. Since it was a Gene Autry movie and we had more than three hours before the next bus back to Heart Mountain, we went in. As we were standing in the line at the refreshment stand, I noticed that a couple of boys who were about my age were giving us long, curious glances. However, nothing was said. Although it was probably no better than average for a small town, I was quite impressed with the Powell movie theater. It had a floor-to-ceiling retractable curtain in front of the screen, large murals of Western scenes on the sidewalls, and an attractive refreshment stand with a gleaming glass display case. The two movie theaters in Heart Mountain had none of these amenities.

After the movie, we still had almost two hours to browse through the town. That would be more than adequate. First, we went into the only department store in the town. It was a small independently-operated store that was little more than half the size of the JC Penny in Kent. Still, compared to the canteen at Heart Mountain, it was quite nice. Giro bought each of us a sweater. I chose an attractive blue sweater in a style that was very popular at the time. The sweater buttoned in the front. The arms and back were a solid blue, but the front was adorned with a colorful checkered pattern. Hank chose a sweater that was identical in every respect, except color. His sweater was brown.

After browsing through the rest of the town and buying a few snacks to take back to Heart Mountain, we went into a small restaurant that appeared to be the best in town. There was a neon sign above the door with large letters at the top that read, "The Powell Cafe." Below that were small letters that read, "The Best in Western Dining."

The dining area of the restaurant consisted of a lunch counter and a half-dozen tables, all of which were covered with bright red and white checkered tablecloths. There was only one customer in the restaurant when we entered. He was a young man in a ten-gallon hat who was sitting at the counter drinking coffee and talking to the waitress behind the counter. The waitress greeted us with a smile, motioned us to a table beside the window, and brought us water. She was a moderately plump, middle-aged woman with rusty red hair. Except for the fact that she did not have freckles, in mannerism and appearance, there was a striking resemblance between her and Mrs. Hannon.

Except for Giro, who ordered coffee for his drink, we all ordered deluxe hamburgers, French fries, and soda water. A deluxe hamburger at the Powell Café consisted of a fresh hamburger patty, lettuce, tomato, onion, sliced pickles, mayonnaise, and sweet mustard sandwiched between halves of a freshly baked bun. At the time, I had no recollection of ever having eaten a hamburger patty on a bun. It is probably impossible to adequately describe to American readers in the twenty-first century just how good such a hamburger would taste to a food-conscious Depression-era adolescent who had been living on relocation center fare for two and a half years.

The Nisei soldier and his lady friend, who turned out to be his fiancée, were waiting at the bus stop in front of the post office when we arrived. The soldier told Giro that he had recently completed the Army Language School at Fort Snelling, Minnesota, and would be reporting to Fort Mason, the port of embarkation in San Francisco, in a few days. He also said that he had no inkling of exactly where he was going or whether he would be assigned to a combat unit or a rear echelon intelligence unit. His fiancée, a demure, attractive young lady, unconsciously took his hand as he said that.

During the week after our outing to Powell, Toshiko and Sam also returned home for a visit with the family. Giro and Sam had originally left the Pinedale Assembly Center in order to work on the sugar beet harvest in Ogden, Utah. Toshiko had left in Tule Lake in January 1943 in order to go to Rochester, Minnesota, where, through her former employer in Seattle, she had obtained employment as a maid for a doctor at the Mayo Clinic. However, like thousands of other young Nisei men and women, all three of them had eventually migrated to Chicago in order to work in defense plants where the working conditions and pay were better.

Toshiko had returned home because she wanted to personally inform my parents that she would soon be marrying Yoshio Katayama, a young man whom she had met through friends in Chicago. Prior to the evacuation, Yoshio had been a strawberry farmer on Bainbridge Island, a small, picturesque island in Puget Sound. At the time of Toshiko's visit, Yoshio's parents were interned in the Minidoka War Relocation Center in Idaho.

It was a long, arduous journey from Chicago to Heart Mountain. The trip began with a two-day train ride to Billings, a small, wheat-and-cattle town in south central Montana. This trip was followed by a dusty four-hour ride on ancient busses that made only two trips each day and stopped at every little hamlet along the way. This included a change of busses at Deaver, Wyoming—population: 150. However, since my parents had never met Yoshio or any other members of the

Katayama family, Toshiko felt that etiquette dictated that she make the trip in order to obtain the blessing of my parents.

Sam had returned for a visit because, like Giro, he had passed his pre-induction physical examination and would also soon be leaving for the Army. Giro and Sam were both patriotic young Americans. Although Sam had still been a senior at Kent High School at the time, both had volunteered for military service shortly after Pearl Harbor. However, they had been rejected for service and classified as enemy aliens by the Selective Service System. After then being imprisoned at Pinedale, their patriotic zeal had waned and they had both decided to wait for the draft.

By the fall of 1944, the all-Japanese American 442nd Regimental Combat Team, which was to gain fame as the most decorated army unit of its size in World War II, was suffering heavy casualties in Europe. Since it was known that the majority of Nisei draftees were being sent to Europe as replacements for the 442nd Regimental Combat Team immediately after completion of basic training, my parents were very concerned that this might be the last opportunity for us to get together as a family. Plans were therefore made to have one last meal together and have a family portrait taken.

Although there were no photo studios in the relocation center, the family portrait was no problem, because there were several professional photographers in Heart Mountain who could take the picture outdoors. The family meal, however, did present a problem, because mess halls could not be used for private purposes and there were no other dining facilities available within the relocation center. It was therefore decided that Mom, with the help of Toshiko and Betty, would make a *sukiyaki* dinner in our quarters. A very understanding crew in the Upper 12 mess hall let us borrow the necessary utensils and gave us very generous rations. This meal was supplemented by purchases from the canteen and appropriations from the project farm where Dad was working.

After a sumptuous meal, we all dressed in our "Sunday best" for the family portrait, which was taken on the gravel road between Upper 12 and Upper 17 with the majestic mountain in the background. My Sunday best consisted of a white shirt, dark corduroy trousers, and my well-worn engineer's boots. Unfortunately, poor Kiku, who had been hospitalized for a tonsillectomy a few days earlier, missed both the meal and the photo session.

◆   ◆   ◆

During the month of September, Heart Mountain was visited by an all-star baseball team from the Gila River Relocation Center in Arizona. The Gila All-Stars played a series of thirteen games against the Heart Mountain All-Stars, as well as squads assembled from some of the better teams in Heart Mountain. They won nine of the thirteen games. In the company of Giro and Sam, who were both sports enthusiasts, I attended many of those games.

The Gila All-Stars were lead by player-manager Kenichi "Pop" Zenimura and his two teenage sons, Harvey and Howard. Kenichi Zenimura, an Issei, had been a prominent promoter of baseball in the Japanese American communities of central California prior to the war. During the 1930s, he had participated in postseason exhibition games against the likes of Babe Ruth and Lou Gehrig, which drew thousands of spectators. After the war, both Harvey and Howard went on to successful professional baseball careers in Japan.

To a large extent, the visit of the Gila All-Stars was financed by passing a hat among the spectators. The Community Affairs Office later reported gross receipts of $1,547.27, an impressive amount considering that the top pay for an evacuee was only nineteen dollars a month.

◆　　◆　　◆

On Monday, the twenty-fifth of September, Heart Mountain High School was closed for two weeks in order to permit students in the upper grades to help with the harvest on the project farm. Members of the faculty also worked on the harvest. The *Heart Mountain Sentinel* later reported that students and faculty had made it possible to harvest a record 120,854 pounds of beans, cabbages, carrots, celery, Chinese cabbages, corn, cucumbers, daikon radishes, green onions, Japanese spinach, lettuce, parsley, peas, potatoes, squash, spinach, and tomatoes.

◆　　◆　　◆

By the first of October, Toshiko, Giro, and Sam had all left Heart Mountain and gone their separate ways. Life returned to normal for me, but only for a few days. On the ninth of the month, Fred departed for New York City on indefinite leave.

When an evacuee such as an agricultural worker left a relocation center on temporary leave with the intention of returning, that person remained in the custody of the War Relocation Authority. However, an evacuee who departed on indefinite leave with the intention of settling outside of the relocation center was released from custody. Such persons were entitled to a relocation allowance of twenty-five dollars, a one-way train ticket to the destination of choice, and a per diem meal allowance of three dollars while en route to the destination of choice. Since jobs were plentiful throughout the country and he was now in reasonably good health, Fred decided he would avail himself of the opportunity to travel and see as much of the country as possible.

With Fred's departure, Harry, who was a senior at Heart Mountain High, became the senior occupant of Room 1217-D. Harry had become fond of Western music while he was in Heart Mountain and was learning to play the guitar. However, although Western music was being played constantly over the radio station in Billings, Montana, in deference to Fred, who preferred classical music and was outspoken in what he did not like, Harry seldom played the radio while Fred was in the room. Following Fred's departure, Hank, Ben, and I, who shared the room with Harry, began to awake each morning to the sound of Bob Nolan and the Sons of the Pioneers singing and playing their immortal hits, "Cool Water" and "Tumbling Tumbleweeds":

> See them tumbling down,
> Pledging their love to the ground.
> Lonely but free I'll be found,
> Drifting along with the tumbling tumbleweeds.
>
> Cares of the past are behind.
> Nowhere to go, but I'll find,
> Just where the trail will wind,
> Drifting along with the tumbling tumbleweeds.
>
> I know when night is gone,
> That a new world's born at dawn.
> I'll keep rolling along,
> Deep in my heart is a song.
> Here on the range I belong,
> Drifting along with the tumbling tumbleweeds.

◆   ◆   ◆

The biggest sporting event in the short history of the relocation center occurred on the fourth of November, when the Casper High School Mustangs made a round trip of almost 450 miles to play a football game against the Heart Mountain Eagles. At a time when gasoline was rationed throughout the country, this was almost unheard of for a high school sporting event. The Heart Mountain Eagles entered the game unbeaten and untied in two seasons of competition against small neighboring high schools. However, this event would be the first time that an athletic team from Heart Mountain High would be playing a team from a larger high school. As a result, there was a tremendous amount of interest in the game, which attracted what was believed to be the largest crowd ever to see an athletic event in northwestern Wyoming.

As the teams went through pre-game warm-up exercises, it appeared that we might be witnessing a mismatch. The Mustangs, lead by a huge, 210-pound all-state fullback, outweighed the Eagles by more than 30 pounds per man. As the Mustangs ran a few pre-game plays, they looked awesome in their colorful orange uniforms, trimmed in black and white. In contrast, the much smaller Eagles looked ragged. Many of the Eagles were wearing baggy pants that were taped around the thigh in order to keep thigh pads in place. They all wore cheap white practice jerseys that had blue numerals stenciled on the back.

The game turned out to be anything but a rout. The Mustangs, taking advantage of their superior size, dominated the middle of the line and concentrated on a powerful running attack from an old-fashioned single-wing offense. Leroy Pearce, their huge all-state fullback, led the way with two touchdowns on short plunges through the middle of the line. The smaller but faster Eagles countered with tricky reverses and sweeps, as well as a wide-open passing attack from their T-formation. Ultimately, the game hinged on a crucial play late in the third quarter, when George "Crazy Legs" Yahiro, the Eagles' star halfback, was unable to handle a hurriedly thrown pass in the end zone. As a result, the Mustangs emerged with a hard-fought 19-13 victory. The game ended with the huge crowd abuzz over the exciting game that they had just witnessed.

◆   ◆   ◆

Monday, November 20, 1944, was the saddest day in the three-year history of Heart Mountain High School. At an assembly of the entire student body and faculty, Principal John K. Corbett announced that over the weekend, the parents of nineteen-year-old Ted Fujioka had been informed that Ted had been killed in action while serving with the 442nd Regimental Combat Team in France. In Ted's honor, the flag at the high school was flown at half-mast that day.

Ted was the first student body president of Heart Mountain High School. It was largely through his effort that the flagpole at an abandoned Civilian Conservation Corps (CCC) camp outside of Powell was relocated to the high school. The flag was first raised at a ceremony on December 22, 1942, with the Heart Mountain Boy Scout Drum and Bugle Corps playing "To the Colors," and Fujioka and Mr. Corbett leading the faculty and students in the Pledge of Allegiance. Mr. Corbett initially had reservations about conducting such a ceremony, because he feared that some of the students might react negatively due to resentment about the way they had been treated by the United States government. However, based largely on Fujioka's assurance that such concerns were not warranted, the ceremony was conducted and proceeded without incidence.

A few weeks later, the original flag-raising ceremony was reenacted for the benefit of famed photographers, Hansel Mieth and her husband, Otto Hagel, who were visiting Heart Mountain on an assignment for *Life* magazine. However, the moving photograph was not published until almost forty years later, when it appeared in *Time* magazine. Evidently, wartime censors had recognized the incongruity of incarcerating innocent, obviously loyal American youths who were raising the American flag up a flagpole that they themselves had erected.

Ted Fujioka volunteered for military service soon after his graduation from Heart Mountain High in July 1943. Following the notification of his death, some bitter supporters of the Fair Play Committee, whose own loved ones were languishing in federal penitentiaries, chided Ted's parents for having allowed their son to sacrifice himself for a cause that was so unworthy. Such spiteful recriminations have contributed to the bitter acrimony that has plagued the Japanese American community for more than fifty years.

◆   ◆   ◆

Based on his academic record for the first six weeks of the school year, my pal and classmate in 7-3, Takuhei "Tak" Iseri was promoted to 7-2. I was happy for him, because I knew that he considered the promotion to be a feather in his bonnet, but I was in no way envious. I was happy in 7-3.

◆   ◆   ◆

On the eighteenth of December, the Supreme Court of the United States announced its ruling in the case of Mitsuye Endo vs. the United States. Ms. Endo was an American of Japanese ancestry from Sacramento, California, who was evacuated from her home in the spring of 1942. In early 1943, during the registration period in Tule Lake, the determination had been made that Ms. Endo was a loyal, law-abiding citizen. She was therefore moved to the relocation center at Topaz, Utah, where she had remained until the date of the Supreme Court ruling.

In this extremely important ruling for Japanese Americans, the Supreme Court had ruled in a unanimous decision that the government could not continue to detain and exclude from specified areas of the country a citizen who had been determined to be loyal and law abiding. In essence, this meant that the government could not continue to detain loyal Japanese Americans and also could not prohibit them from returning to their homes on the West Coast. In some circles, it is thought that in the case of Mitsuye Endo vs. the United States, the Supreme Court had ruled that the evacuation had been unconstitutional. Such is not the case. The Supreme Court ruled only that the government could not continue to detain and segregate a citizen after that citizen had been administratively determined to be a loyal, law-abiding citizen.

On the day before the Supreme Court ruling, the War Department announced that, effective January 2, 1945, it had rescinded General DeWitt's Proclamation Number 1 and a series of exclusion orders that followed. These orders had designated the West Coast as a sensitive military area and provided for the removal of all persons of Japanese ancestry from the region. The action of the War Department in rescinding the orders was based on prior knowledge of the Supreme Court ruling that was a foregone conclusion. The evacuation had been justified by the Western Defense Command in early 1942 as a military necessity due to the threat of invasion and the impossibility of quickly determining the loyalty of individual Japanese Americans. The threat of invasion no longer existed, and the loyalty of Ms. Endo had been established. What possible justification, other than her Japanese ancestry, existed to continue to detain and exclude her?

A few days after the Supreme Court ruling in the Endo Case, it was reported in the *Heart Mountain Sentinel* that all relocation centers except Tule Lake, which was now known as a "segregation center," would be closed before the end of 1945. It was also announced that the War Relocation Authority itself would be disbanded and cease to exist after June 30, 1946.

At first, news of the closing of the relocation centers was received calmly in Heart Mountain. After all, it was obvious to almost everyone that the war was drawing to a close. A few days later, however, a groundswell of anger and resentment began to surface in all of the relocation centers, especially among the Issei. The overwhelming majority of Issei had accepted evacuation peacefully as an unfortunate event over which they had no control. All had lost their freedom and most had lost almost everything that they had owned. Ironically, now that freedom was about to be thrust back upon them, many of the Issei began to protest openly. Meetings were held and representatives were sent to voice their concerns to camp administrators. Delegates from Heart Mountain were even sent to Salt Lake City in order to meet with representatives from the other relocation centers.

Opposition to the sudden closing of the relocation centers was based largely on two factors. First, the timing was horrible. With the war still in progress, many of the Issei were worried about being forced out into an environment that they perceived to be hostile. These fears were heightened when reporters began to filter back to the relocation centers news that some of the first evacuees to return to their former homes on the West Coast had been the victims of violence, including arson and shootings.

The primary concern, however, was economic. Most of the Issei were now in their late fifties or sixties. Having lost most of their assets due to the evacuation, many were virtually penniless and had neither the resources nor the energy to start over from scratch. Worse still, there were no homes or jobs waiting for them, and the government was offering a measly twenty-five-dollar allowance to start life anew. The problem was especially acute for aging bachelors and couples who had no children to help them get reestablished on the outside. How could they possibly survive on the pittance that the War Relocation Authority would give them as an allowance when they left the relocation centers? It was proposed that the evacuees refuse to leave en masse until a more reasonable amount was offered. A few of the Issei were so pessimistic about their prospects on the outside that they resolved to simply refuse to be evicted from the relocation center.

◆   ◆   ◆

Early in January, the Community Service Office presented my mother with a white satin pennant that was trimmed with a red border and contained two big blue stars. She proudly displayed this pennant, which was known as the "Sons in Service" flag, in the window of her room.

◆   ◆   ◆

Along with thirty-five other seniors, Harry graduated from Heart Mountain as a mid-term graduate on January 19, 1945. Mid-term graduates completed their schooling five months ahead of their classmates by carrying extra-credit courses.

Included among the mid-term graduates was Harry's pal, Bob Yamamoto, who also lived in Upper 12. Bob was a tall, handsome young man who prior to the war had lived in Renton, a small town at the north end of the White River Valley. Soon after graduation, Bob relocated to eastern Oregon. While in Oregon, Bob volunteered for military service, against the wishes of his father who was still in Heart Mountain. However, he failed to pass his physical examination and did not serve until many years later, when he was drafted during the Korean War. Ironically, Harry, who had no intention of volunteering, was drafted later in the year.

It turned out that Harry's decision to carry extra-credit classes and graduate ahead of his classmates was not a wise one. He had no job waiting for him and absolutely no plans for the immediate future. At the time, high school students were being considered by the Selective Service System only if there was indication that graduation was being deliberately delayed in order to avoid the draft. Therefore, by remaining in school until the end of the school year, Harry would have avoided the possibility of being drafted for an additional five months.

◆   ◆   ◆

As one might expect under the circumstances, there was pent up resentment against Caucasians among a significant segment of the evacuee population in the relocation centers. At Heart Mountain High, this resentment was especially evident among students with older brothers who had been imprisoned during the previous summer because of their support for the Fair Play Committee. For the most part, this resentment was not directed against individual members of the faculty at the high school. There were exceptions, however.

In early February, Miss Rayburn (pseudonym), my English teacher, who had joined the faculty at the start of the school year, abruptly left and was replaced by Mr. Nelson. Miss Rayburn was a pleasant, well-meaning young lady but seemed to lack the experience and firmness of personality that was needed to maintain order in a classroom full of boisterous seventh graders. It was rumored that she had resigned due to stress.

The problem began for Miss Rayburn virtually at the start of the school year, when it became obvious that she lacked firmness in quelling minor disturbances in the classroom. Soon these disturbances escalated into backtalk and eventually open rebellion in the classroom. I personally liked Miss Rayburn and was sympathetic to her plight. I could not understand why she failed to send a couple of the worst offenders to the principal's office. At a time when corporal punishment was not unknown in schools, a trip to the principal's office would probably have solved Miss Rayburn's problems. If corporal punishment failed to resolve the problem, calling the parents of the offending students in to the principal's office, or even merely threatening to do so, certainly would have resolved the problem. The Issei had great respect for educators, and the Nisei all understood that. No Nisei student would have dared risk subjecting an Issei parent to the humiliation of being called to school for a meeting with the principal.

One of Miss Rayburn's most persistent and abusive tormentors was Ray (pseudonym), one of the biggest and toughest kids in the class. Ray had an older brother who was among the imprisoned Fair Play Committee supporters. Along with a couple of his friends, Ray constantly harassed poor Miss Rayburn about the racism Japanese Americans suffered at the hands of white people. One day, Ray attacked Miss Rayburn with the charge that the Nisei were being forced to bear the brunt of the fighting in Europe and the Nisei were winning the war against Germany virtually single-handedly. Taken aback by such a ridiculous charge, Miss Rayburn responded with incredulity: "Oh, Ray, that simply is not true."

This was not an isolated case of a poorly informed adolescent in Heart Mountain harboring such a distorted view of the 442nd Regimental Combat Team's importance in the overall American war effort in Europe. The *Heart Mountain Sentinel* and the *Pacific Citizen*, the official publication of the JACL, were the only newspapers that were being widely circulated in Heart Mountain. Both were full of stories about the heroic exploits of the 442nd Regimental Combat Team and the heavy casualties that were being suffered by the men of the 442nd.

◆   ◆   ◆

On the night of the thirteenth of February, Heart Mountain High School concluded three years of athletic competition against neighboring high schools with a 42-20 victory over the Cody Broncs basketball team. In spite of winning the last four games by wide margins, the Eagles finished the 1944–45 basketball season with a record of six wins and four losses, not impressive considering the fact that all of the neighboring schools were much smaller than Heart Mountain High.

♦   ♦   ♦

One day in early March, Hank and I engaged in our last fistfight. Hank was fifteen months older than I was, but we were approximately the same size. He was, however, stronger, faster, and more athletic. For the most part, we had a friendly relationship and played well together with the other boys in Upper 12. As might be expected, however, we also had occasional differences, and these differences sometimes resulted in physical skirmishes. Hank always won handily.

There was not a mean bone in Hank's body. He never inflicted unnecessary punishment on me. When it became obvious that I had been defeated and had learned my lesson for the moment, the fight was over and the incident was soon forgotten. These beatings did grate on my mind, however, and I decided that I had to put a stop to them. I realized that because I was afraid of him, Hank always got in the first punch. Obviously, he also got in the last punch. I therefore made up my mind that the next time Hank got ready to hit me, I would beat him to the punch, literally.

The fight took place on a warm, sunny afternoon. Hank and I, along with a couple of friends from the neighborhood, were playing with Harry's barbells. We called them barbells, but they were not real barbells. Harry, who was a bodybuilding enthusiast, had made a set of exercise weights by filling two one-gallon cans with concrete and connecting the cans with a steel pipe, which had also been filled with concrete.

Hank and I got into an argument over whose turn it was to use the weights. The argument soon became heated, and I was sure that Hank was going to punch me in the face. I was ready. Without hesitation, I punched him as hard as I could. He reeled backward, tripped over the handle of the weights, and fell to the ground. More surprised than hurt, he began to get up. I knew that if he got up and took a fighting stance, I was a dead duck, so I rushed forward over the barbell and threw a haymaker. It landed squarely on his nose. This one was a clean knockdown and sent him sprawling back to the ground. He lay there on his back, momentarily stunned by the force of the punch. I had no idea that I was capable of hitting anyone with such force. Obviously, the fact that he was still getting up and was somewhat off balance when I hit him had much to do with the effectiveness of the punch.

Suddenly, red with blood and rage, Hank tackled me and wrestled me to the ground. We were rolling in the dirt, cursing and trying to punch each other in the face, when Harry heard the commotion and came outside to pull us apart. Hank was a mess. He was bleeding profusely from the nose and was covered with dirt and blood. I was also dirty and bloody. There is no doubt in my mind that if Harry had not stopped the fight, Hank would have given me the beating of my life because he was positively livid. That did not deter me. I was determined and had made up my mind that I was not going to take it anymore.

Hank and I continued to have our differences, but this turned out to be the very last time that we ever engaged in a fistfight. The reason was not because of any fear on Hank's part. Hank was a tough little guy. There was no reason for him to fear any boy of his size in Heart Mountain, least of all me. We both knew that in a fair fight, he could whip me any day of the week. However, Hank also realized that I was no longer afraid of him and was prepared to defend my own turf.

A few days after the fight, Harry left on indefinite leave for Burns, Oregon, where he went to work as a laborer on a railroad section gang.

◆　　◆　　◆

On the night of Saturday, March 4, the Heart Mountain Police Force conducted a raid on a gambling establishment in Upper 22. News of the raid resulted in much commotion and laughter throughout the relocation center, when it was later reported in the *Heart Mountain Sentinel* that Mr. Kiyoichi Doi had been among the twenty-three men that had been apprehended by the police. Mr. Doi was the widely respected Issei chairman of the Heart Mountain Judicial Commission, which was responsible for meting out punishment for minor infractions within the relocation center.

◆　　　◆　　　◆

In a banner front-page article, the *Heart Mountain Sentinel* reported on March 24 that the Bureau of Reclamation had leased to local farmers all farmlands that had previously been cultivated as part of the project vegetable farm. The article also reported that this was the first concrete evidence that the relocation center would soon be closing. In an accompanying article, it was reported that Project Director Guy Robertson had urged all appointed (Caucasian) staff to assist in the final relocation of evacuees by consolidating and eliminating non-essential evacuee positions. Presumably, unemployed evacuees in Heart Mountain would need less prodding to relocate.

◆　　　◆　　　◆

In late April, I met my brother-in-law, Yoshio Katayama, for the first time, when he and Toshiko stopped in Heart Mountain for a brief visit while en route from Chicago to Tooele, Utah, where they were going to work at an Army ordnance depot. Yoshio, a short, husky man, greeted me with a smile and a firm handshake. He impressed me as a likeable, pleasant man; but, like many Nisei men, he was somewhat reserved.

Toshiko and Yosh were driving across the country in a green 1941 International pick-up truck, which the Katayama family had purchased in the summer of 1941. When Japanese Americans were evacuated from Bainbridge Island in early 1942, the pick-up was stored with a friendly Caucasian neighbor. After evacuees had been cleared to voluntarily relocate to areas outside of the West Coast military zone, the pick-up was driven to the Minidoka War Relocation Center by an understanding Christian minister. Yosh then drove the pick-up to Chicago, where he took up temporary residence. Yosh was a "chick-sexer," a skilled technician trained to quickly and accurately separate, newly-hatched chicks by sex. A vehicle was a necessity for Yosh, because he was required to travel quite extensively through rural areas of the Midwest during the chick-hatching season, which was in the late fall and early winter.

◆   ◆   ◆

News of the unconditional surrender of Germany on May 7, 1945, was met with great relief throughout Heart Mountain. By then, hundreds of men from the relocation centers were in the armed forces, many with the 442nd Regimental Combat Team, which was continuing to suffer heavy casualties. Almost every issue of the *Heart Mountain Sentinel* contained at least one article about men from Heart Mountain who had been wounded or killed in action in Europe.

Less well-publicized was the fact that casualties were also being incurred by Japanese American servicemen in the Pacific. Thousands of Nisei, as well as Kibei (Americans of Japanese ancestry educated in Japan), were serving as translators and intelligence analysts in the Pacific Theater of Operations. These men were assigned to all branches of the U.S. Armed Forces. A few were even assigned to serve with the armed forces of allied nations. Some senior military officers later expressed the opinion that the information that these men obtained by intercepting radio messages and interrogating prisoners may have shortened the war against Japan by as much as two years. However, due to military censorship, little publicity was given to the extremely important contribution of these men until many years after the end of World War II.

◆   ◆   ◆

On May 25, 1945, Heart Mountain High School closed its doors for the last time. At most schools, the last day of the school year is a time for rejoicing. This was not a day for rejoicing at Heart Mountain High. Many of the students had been living together almost like siblings for almost three years, and unique bonds of friendship had been forged. Soon, these friends would be scattered across the country, perhaps never to see one another again. Almost all of the students faced an uncertain future with parents who had been impoverished by the evacuation. Many of the students had also formed warm relationships with their teachers, who were for the most part, sincere, dedicated educators who fully understood the difficult times that the evacuees were about to face. More than a few students left for home that day on the verge of tears.

◆   ◆   ◆

With the end of the school year, the number of evacuees leaving Heart Mountain began to slowly increase. For the most part, those departing early were the small number of evacuees who owned property on the West Coast. This consisted largely of farmers, nurserymen, and operators of small hotels on skid row. Inhibited from leaving early were some of the most industrious men in the relocation center. These were the men who had operated businesses in Japanese American communities prior to the war. Not knowing which communities would be reestablished and fearing boycott by the general public, their concerns were legitimate. Of the roughly one hundred Japanese families that had resided in the Kent area prior to the war, little more than ten percent returned after the war. This low rate of return was largely attributable to the fact that many of the former residents had already relocated to Idaho and eastern Oregon. Another important factor was the poor economic prospects in the White River Valley due to the short growing season in western Washington.

Because very few families in Upper 12 were among those that departed early, the summer of 1945 began in much the same manner as the previous summer. My friends and I went to the swimming pool almost every afternoon. Our interest in baseball having increased due to the visit of the Gila River All-Stars during the previous season, on weekends, we also went to several baseball games.

The most popular baseball team in Heart Mountain was the San Jose Zebras. The Zebras had a large following, because they were the most successful team in the relocation center and also because a large segment of the population in Heart Mountain was from Santa Clara County, California. My favorite team, however, was the Heart Mountain Amateurs, a team that was made up primarily of former Washingtonians from the small central-Washington town of Wapato. Although former Washingtonians accounted for only a small percentage of the population in Heart Mountain, the Amateurs were one of the strongest teams in the relocation center. The success of the team was largely attributable to their star pitcher, George Iseri, who was generally considered the best pitcher in Heart Mountain. George was the older brother of Yukio "Yubo" Iseri, Ben's frequent accomplice in petty mischief as a third grader at Washington Elementary School.

During the summer of 1945, Hank and I became interested in building crystal sets though Hank's friend Kohachi Toyota. A crystal set is a simple radio-listening device that makes it possible to pick up radio broadcasts through earphones. Kohachi had a subscription to *Popular Science*, which periodically published schematic drawings of crystal sets and simple radios. Using parts that had been ordered from a mail-order catalog, Kohachi would build a simple receiver, then sell it in order to finance a more sophisticated set.

Kohachi helped Hank and me build our first set, which we shared amicably. Basically, it consisted of earphones, a crystal detecting device, and a coil that we had fashioned by wrapping fine copper wire around the core of a roll of toilet paper. Because it was not equipped with a tuner, it did not have the capacity to separate signals if more than one station was transmitting in the area. However, since the radio station in Billings was the only one in the area, our crude crystal set worked quite well in Heart Mountain.

Kohachi was a bright, studious kid who had been in Homeroom 8-1 during the previous school year. Just as I had few friends in 7-1, Hank had few friends in 8-1. However, Kohachi was an exception, because he and Hank had been friends and classmates in the first grade.

Prior to the spring of 1938, when my family moved to Kent, my dad had farmed a small plot of land in the foothills of the Cascade Mountains, just east of Kent. Kohachi's father had farmed the adjacent plot. In the fall of 1937, Hank and Kohachi began school together as first graders at the Panther Lake Elementary School. A short while before we moved to Kent, the Toyota family moved to Maryhill, a small agricultural community just north of the Columbia River in central Washington. They had renewed their friendship as seventh graders at Heart Mountain High in the fall of 1943.

◆   ◆   ◆

Late one afternoon in early July, my friends and I came home from the swimming pool to find many of the residents of Upper 12 looking up into the bright afternoon sky. They were looking at a strange light high up in the sky. It was not moving and looked like a small star. A star in the bright afternoon sky? Impossible! There was a great deal of speculation about what it might be. One might have speculated that it was a flying saucer, except that at that time, nobody had ever heard of a flying saucer. To the ridicule of the Nisei, some of the Issei, who against all logic were still holding out hope for a Japanese victory, speculated that it was a secret Japanese weapon. Why would the Japanese send a secret weapon to hover over a harmless, half-deserted camp out in the middle of the prairie? The mysterious light was no longer there the next day and the incident was soon forgotten.

◆   ◆   ◆

On the thirteenth of July, Dillon S. Myer, Director of the War Relocation Authority in Washington, D.C., announced the closing dates for all relocation centers except Tule Lake, which was now known as a segregation center. The closing date for Tule Lake could not be determined until after the war, because it was known that many of the evacuees in Tule Lake would be repatriated to Japan after the war. The scheduled closing date for Heart Mountain was November 15, just four months and two days after the date of the announcement. In an article that appeared in the next issue of the *Heart Mountain Sentinel*, Project Director Guy Robertson warned residents that the November 15 closing date was firm, and that all facilities, including the hospital and all mess halls, would be closed on or before that date. Residents were therefore urged to report to the administrative office in order to finalize departure plans.

On the twenty-sixth of July, Johnny Kawasaki, my young friend in Barrack 1218 who was originally from Los Angeles, departed with his family for Cleveland, Ohio. Johnny was the first of my close friends in Upper 12 to leave the relocation center.

◆   ◆   ◆

On Saturday, July 18, 1945, the *Heart Mountain Sentinel* published its final edition and passed into history. It was replaced by a mimeograph *Sentinel Supplement*, which was published whenever necessary to disseminate essential information to evacuees remaining in the relocation center.

The *Sentinel* was an eight-page, tabloid-size newspaper that was published for less than three years. In addition to the eight-page

English-language section, there was a Japanese-language section. At its peak, the *Sentinel* had a circulation of 6,000. Postal workers in Heart Mountain reported that as many as 4,500 copies were being mailed each week to readers outside of the relocation center after first having been read by the original purchasers. Because the *Sentinel* was printed at a commercial print shop and was led from the date of inception to the last day of operation by professional journalists, it was considered to be by far the best and most influential of the newspapers published in a relocation center. I personally read the *Sentinel*, especially the sports pages, on a regular basis. At two cents per copy, it was among the best bargains in the relocation center.

Because the brightest and best-qualified among the evacuees tended to be among the first to leave the relocation center, the *Sentinel* staff suffered a turnover of almost five hundred percent during its short lifetime. Despite this horrendous turnover rate, the *Sentinel* maintained its high standards and staunch pro-JACL posture to the very end.

The *Sentinel* has been oft times criticized, especially in recent years, for its seemingly servile attitude toward the War Relocation Authority. At times, this criticism has amounted to a charge that the *Sentinel* staff sold out fellow Japanese Americans in order to curry favor with the government. Such charges are ludicrous. *Sentinel* staffers were paid the standard sixteen dollars a month. They also lived in the same dingy barracks and ate the same lousy mess hall food as the rest of us.

Like the JACL, the *Heart Mountain Sentinel* was dominated by thoughtful, conscientious young men and women who believed that the future of Japanese Americans was in the United States. They believed that the most effective way to combat the racists and self-serving politicians who gained the upper hand as a result of the hysteria following Pearl Harbor was to win over the American public with an undeniable demonstration of loyalty. For them, there was no other viable option. For people of color, life in the so-called Western Democracies was far from perfect, but at least there was hope for the future. Nazi Germany and Imperial Japan made no secret of their vile intentions. As Americans who truly believed in democracy, Japanese Americans could not in good conscience do anything that might contribute to a victory by the Axis Powers.

It is true that the *Sentinel* did support such controversial actions as the formation of a segregated all-Japanese American combat unit and the drafting of the Nisei from the relocation centers. It is not true, however, that the *Sentinel* mindlessly supported all actions and policies of the government, even if such actions or policies were unfair or detrimental to evacuees in the relocation centers. In the issue of November 14, 1942, the *Sentinel* criticized a War Relocation Authority directive that prohibited Issei from serving on self-governing boards and commissions in the relocation centers. In the very next issue, the *Sentinel* reported fully and fairly in a banner front-page article, widespread unrest in Heart Mountain over a plan to enclose the relocation center with barbed-wire fences and guard towers. A review of microfilm copies of the *Sentinel* indicates that these were not isolated cases in which the War Relocation Authority was depicted in a less than favorable light.

It is also not true that the *Sentinel* muffled dissent. The publication was full of letters of complaint. Most of these complaints pertained to such inconveniences as the lack of privacy, crying babies next door, and the poor food in the mess halls. However, in March 1944, the *Sentinel* published long letters from leaders of the Fair Play Committee that they had received in response to an earlier editorial criticizing the committee.

Neither can it be said that members of the *Sentinel* staff were armchair quarterbacks. Sixteen young men who had at one time been associated with the *Sentinel* served in the armed forces during the war. Three, including Ted Fujioka, who was mentioned earlier, were killed in action while serving with the 442nd Regimental Combat Team in Europe. Private First Class Fred Yamamoto, another former student leader at Heart Mountain High School and the first man to volunteer from Heart Mountain, was posthumously awarded the Silver Star for gallantry in action near Biffontaine, France, in October 1944. The third fatality was First Lieutenant Hitoshi "Moe" Yonemura, honor graduate and former head cheerleader at UCLA.

◆   ◆   ◆

On the first of August, the War Relocation Authority issued Administrative Order Number 289. This order authorized project directors in the relocation centers to unilaterally schedule departures for any evacuees who had failed to make plans for departure at least six weeks prior to the scheduled closing of the relocation centers. Such persons were to be returned to the point from which the individual had been evacuated in the spring of 1942.

The War Relocation Authority was widely criticized for this cold-hearted policy, which would virtually throw aging, impoverished evacuees who had already suffered so much out of the relocation centers with a token relocation allowance of only twenty-five dollars. Dillon S. Myer, in his account of the evacuation, *Uprooted Americans*, acknowledged that it was necessary to actually push evacuees into some of the last trains leaving relocation centers. This pushing had not been necessary three and a half years earlier, when these same men and women had been forced from their homes and imprisoned.

For the most part, the criticism came from church leaders and the evacuees themselves. However, considerable criticism also came from within the ranks of the War Relocation Authority. Mr. Myer later dismissed this criticism, claiming it had come from "lower echelon people" and two project directors who might have been motivated by self-interest. Many employees of the War Relocation Authority, especially teachers who remained on the payroll after the end of the school year in order to assist in the administrative task of closing the relocation centers, were dedicated public servants who were interested only in doing whatever they could to help evacuees who had been so grievously wronged. For Mr. Myer to malign former subordinates in this manner is difficult to comprehend.

◆   ◆   ◆

On the second of August, my best friend and constant companion, Ken Murata, departed for New Plymouth, Idaho, a small agricultural community along the Oregon border. During the war, a large number of families that had formerly resided in the White River Valley settled in the area around New Plymouth. In fact, the number of former White River Valley residents that settled in that area greatly exceeded the number that returned to the valley after the war. I never corresponded with Ken after he left Heart Mountain, but for many years, my sister Kiku corresponded with Ken's sister Chizuko.

Kiku had taken much good-natured teasing from her friends about Ken. There are forty-six prefectures in Japan. In the Japanese language, a prefecture is known as a *ken*. Just as Americans refer to themselves as Californians, Washingtonians, etc., the Japanese refer to themselves as Hiroshima-ken, Okinawa-ken, etc. Since my parents were originally from Hiroshima Ken, members of my family were Hiroshima-ken. However, Kiku's friends insisted that she was not Hiroshima-ken, but Murata-ken.

◆   ◆   ◆

News of the unconditional surrender of Japan on August 14, 1945, was received very quietly in Heart Mountain. The overwhelming majority of the Nisei had foreseen the defeat of Japan for a long time. For them, news of the surrender was very good news; it was a chance to get on with life. In deference to the Issei, however, there were no boisterous demonstrations or outward signs of joy in the relocation center. There was, however, a great sense of relief among all evacuees who had relatives in the Army, because there had been rumors that the War

Department was preparing to send the 442nd Regimental Combat Team to the Pacific in order to participate in the invasion of Japan.

The reaction of the Issei to news of the surrender was mixed. Like almost all other immigrants, the Issei had strong emotional ties to their motherland. A few of the Issei, especially bachelors and the childless couples who had not developed ties to the United States, refused to believe that Japan had been defeated. They had been taught that Japan had never lost a war and would never be defeated. Against all logic, some continued to harbor hopes for a Japanese victory to the bitter end. Most, however, were far more rational and received news of the surrender stoically. My father and mother received news of the surrender not with joy but with a great sense of relief. Giro, Sam, and Harry were already in the Army, and Fred expected to be drafted soon.

◆　　◆　　◆

On the seventh of September, my sixteen-year-old sister, Betty, left for Seattle, Washington, in the company of her longtime friend, Myrtle Kumashiro. At Toshiko's request, Dr. Bannick, her pre-war employer, had made arrangements for the two girls to work as live-in babysitters and mothers' helpers while completing high school. Neither Betty nor Myrtle had ever met their new employer, but both were medical doctors and colleagues of Dr. Bannick. There was therefore little anxiety on the part of the parents in allowing such young girls to leave the relocation center unaccompanied.

At the time that the two girls left for Seattle, neither the Kumashiro family nor the Nakagawa family had decided on a relocation site. In late October, the Kumashiro family left for Albuquerque, New Mexico.

◆   ◆   ◆

By the middle of September, Heart Mountain was a rapidly dying community. All recreational facilities, except one of the two movie theaters, had been closed. All organized sports had been discontinued. Mess halls were rapidly being consolidated and each week, a special train carrying four or five hundred evacuees would leave the relocation center. Still, many of the evacuees were unable to decide what to do or where to go.

The Nakagawa family was among hundreds of families in Heart Mountain that had still not decided what to do. My older siblings were scattered across the country. Sister Toshiko was on Bainbridge Island, Washington, with her husband and infant daughter. They were sharing a house with in-laws and working to restore the Katayama strawberry farm, which had been neglected since the spring of 1942. My five older brothers were either in the Army or in a transitional state themselves. Except for small Army dependence checks, there was little that they could do to help.

A very important consideration for my parents was the need to get Hank, Kiku, Ben, and me back into school. In most of the Western states, the school year began on the day after Labor Day. We were therefore already late for the start of the school year, and everybody was concerned. By word of mouth, we had learned that none of our close friends were planning to return to the White River Valley. Of our three closest Japanese neighbors prior to the war, the Nakatsuka family eventually relocated to Denver, Colorado, the Nakashige family to Ogden, Utah, and the Sasaki family to Richmond, California.

Farming was the only occupation in which Dad had expertise. On the advice of some men with whom he had worked on the project farm, Dad gave serious thought to relocating the family to Santa Clara County, California. The big selling point for Santa Clara County was that in California, it is possible to work a farm throughout the year, whereas in Washington State, the growing season is little more than six months. After much soul searching, Santa Clara County was rejected, because Dad was not familiar with the area and had no idea how to get started in a strange environment with no capital and no relatives or close friends. A further deterrent was Dad's age. At almost sixty years of age, Dad no longer felt that he had the energy to start again, virtually from scratch.

In the end, like many of the other evacuees that remained in Heart Mountain, Dad decided to do nothing and let the War Relocation Authority evict us. This was not an act of defiance but one of practicality. There was little point in returning to Kent. There was nothing there for us except some old household goods and farm tools that had been left unguarded in a barn for three and a half years. We had no idea what, if anything, remained. Also, the fall harvest was virtually over, and he knew that there would be no housing available for us in Kent. If some other location was requested, Dad feared that we would be transported to the requested location, given a one-hundred-and-fifty-dollar relocation allowance for the six of us and left to our own resources.

As it turned out, Dad was correct in assuming that since the War Relocation Authority had established a temporary field office in Seattle, the closest location to Kent where housing would be available, we would be sent there. In late September, we were informed that arrangements were being made to relocate us to Seattle sometime in October. Dad was assured that housing would be available but was also told that it was impossible to arrange for employment. It was assumed by all concerned that because thousands of men and women were being laid off at defense plants in the Seattle area, employment prospects for an aging, unskilled Japanese alien who spoke very little English and had just been released from a government detention facility would be bleak.

On the twenty-eighth of September, my next-door neighbor, Tamo Nishimura, departed with his family for Los Angeles, the pre-war home of the Nishimura family. With the departure of the Nishimuras, we were the last family remaining in Barrack 17. When we moved to Heart Mountain two years earlier, there had been four other families in the barrack.

A few days after the departure of the Nishimura family, the Upper 12 mess hall was closed and it became necessary to use the mess hall in Lower 17, which was some 500 feet farther from our quarters. The closing of the Upper 12 mess hall was not entirely bad, however. Because the Toyota family lived in Lower 17, Hank and I were now able to have our meals with our pal Kohachi Toyota. The Toyota family, which consisted of eight members, had originally been given only one room in Upper 15. However, as the population in Heart Mountain began to decline in the fall of 1944, they moved to Lower 17, where they were given an additional room.

In early October, the transportation office notified us that we would be leaving for Seattle later in the month. It was great news for me. Heart Mountain had become such a boring, depressing place that all I could think about was getting out of there as soon as possible. Almost all of my friends had either already departed or had received firm departure dates. The weather was turning cold and there was nothing to do. Many of the barracks were completely empty and most of the mess halls had been closed. Adding to the gloom was the fact that the relocation center was very dark at night, because there was no light coming from the empty barracks, and many of the streetlights were out, because routine maintenance had been discontinued. They were not even replacing burned-out light bulbs in the bathrooms. In order to get replacement light bulbs for the bathrooms, some evacuees were starting to take light bulbs that had been left behind in empty barracks.

Another thing that was troubling me was the nagging sense that I needed to get back to school. I was very concerned about how I would be received by students and faculty at my next school, but I was also worried about missing so much of the next school year that I might be required to repeat the eighth grade. Quite naturally, I was also worried about my family's bleak economic prospects. Like any normal thirteen-year-old, I was fully aware that things like food, clothing, and housing cost money. I was also aware that my family had virtually no money, and I had never heard of public welfare. I worried about how we were going to survive on the outside.

On the sixteenth of October, my young friends Donald and Akira Ikeda, who lived in Barrack 1218 directly in front of us, left Heart Mountain and returned to their pre-war home in Los Angeles. With the departure of the Ikeda family, Barrack 1218 was completely empty.

After the departure of the Ikeda family, it became necessary for either Hank or me to escort Ben to the bathroom at night, because he was afraid to go by himself after dark. The only light in the immediate area between the two barracks was the light that came from the window of Room 1217-C, where Mom, Dad, and Kiku were staying, and the window of Room 1217-D, which Hank, Ben, and I were sharing. For Ben, more troubling than the darkness was the fact that the bathroom was sometimes empty and eerily quiet at night.

I didn't mind at all when Ben would ask me to go to the bathroom with him. In fact, I welcomed it. After having been constantly among a large number of others for three and a half years, I too thought that it was spooky to be alone in an eerily quiet bathroom at night. I was a child who frequently awoke in the middle of the night because I needed to use the bathroom. On such occasions during my last two weeks in Heart Mountain, I took to doing my business in the shadows of Barrack 1217 rather than going all the way to the bathroom.

On the night of Thursday, October 18, the last motion picture was shown in Heart Mountain. It was a showing of the musical comedy, *Here Come the Waves*, starring Bing Crosby, Betty Hutton, and Sunny Tufts. I did not attend. With the closing of the movie theater, the only facilities remaining in the relocation center to serve the evacuees were a few mess halls, the administrative offices that were processing evacuees for departure, and the hospital. Out of a sense of obligation to the mostly elderly Issei that remained in the relocation center, a handful of dedicated medical professionals remained in Heart Mountain and manned the hospital until the day that the relocation center closed.

On the twenty-fourth of October, Kohachi Toyota left for Chicago, Illinois, on Special Train Number 17 with his mother, three sisters, and two brothers. There they would rejoin Mr. Toyota, who had left the relocation center in May. Like many husbands and fathers, Mr. Toyota had left Heart Mountain ahead of his family in order to find a suitable location to which he might relocate them. Mr. Toyota had initially gone to Cleveland, Ohio; however, not finding Cleveland to his liking, he had moved to Chicago before sending for his family. Mr. Toyota had reservations about Chicago as a suitable future home for his family; however, with Heart Mountain scheduled to close in November, he had no alternative. Had he not done so, War Relocation Authority officials in Heart Mountain would probably have sent the family back to Maryhill, Washington, in accordance with Administrative Order Number 289.

On the same day that Kohachi left for Chicago, the transportation office released the passenger list for Special Train Number 18, which was scheduled to leave Heart Mountain on the thirtieth of the month. The list included the names of the six members of my family who were still in Heart Mountain, as well as approximately four hundred other evacuees who were bound for the Pacific Northwest, northern California, and points east. The transportation office also announced that Special Train Number 20, the last train that was scheduled to transport evacuees out of Heart Mountain, would depart for southern California sometime between the ninth and the thirteenth of November. The train actually left on the tenth.

There was a great deal of confusion in Heart Mountain during its last few weeks of operation. Many of the evacuees had been unable or unwilling to decide upon a relocation site. Housing, especially on the West Coast, where most of the evacuees were destined, was in short supply. Although the fighting had ended in August, the demand for rail transportation was still very high, and the War Relocation Authority did not have a high priority. In spite of these problems, Dillon S. Myer, National Director of the War Relocation Authority, was later able to note with pride that all relocation centers had been closed on or ahead of schedule. Latter-day wags have noted that in quickly emptying eight relocation centers in 1945, Dillon Myer's War Relocation Authority had demonstrated the same cold-hearted efficiency that General DeWitt's Western Defense Command had demonstrated three and a half years earlier in building and filling fifteen assembly centers.

◆　　　◆　　　◆

I left Heart Mountain exactly on schedule, at seven-thirty in the evening on October 30, 1945. It was a clear, moonless night on the prairie. Almost mysteriously, the camp that had looked so dark and gloomy from within glistened against the backdrop of the low rolling hills to the west. As the train left the railroad siding and headed northeast towards Billings, Montana, I was excited and happy to be leaving Heart Mountain but well aware of the fact that difficult times were ahead for my family and me. However, only an extremely dimwitted thirteen-year-old could have been unaware of that fact.

EPILOGUE

On December 23, 1947, President Harry S. Truman granted full pardons to the 267 Japanese Americans who had refused induction into the armed forces from the relocation centers during World War II. This included all former members of the Heart Mountain Fair Play Committee. However, the former Fair Play Committee members had already been freed from federal penitentiaries on an individual basis in 1946.

◆　　　◆　　　◆

On July 2, 1948, President Truman signed into law the Japanese American Evacuation Claims Act of 1948. The act allowed former evacuees to file claims against the United States Government for property losses incurred as a result of the evacuation. It was not however, a generous act. Payment was authorized only for losses that could be documented, and payment was to be based on 1942 values, with no allowance for inflation or interest. Because few evacuees were able to produce adequate documentation to verify losses sustained during the hectic days of early 1942, the vast majority of claims were settled by a compromise with the Department of Justice. On claims that were settled by compromise, payment was limited to $2,500 or seventy-five percent of the original claims, whichever was less. As a result, payments to former evacuees totaled only $38,000,000, which was ten percent of the amount of the property loss that had been estimated by the Federal Reserve Bank.

The Evacuation Claims Act made no provision to compensate former evacuees for the hardships they had incurred as a result of the loss of freedom and income during their years of incarceration.

◆   ◆   ◆

Due in large measure to the skillful stewardship of the five Japanese American members of Congress, in early 1980, both the Senate and the House of Representatives passed bills providing for the establishment of a commission to review the facts surrounding the evacuation and recommend possible remedies. These bills later became known as the Commission on Wartime Relocation and Internment of Civilians Act. The bill was signed into law by President Jimmy Carter on July 31, 1980.

In December 1982, the nine-member commission, which included such highly respected figures as Arthur J. Goldberg, former Supreme Court justice; Edward W. Brooke, former Republican senator from Massachusetts; and Dr. Arthur S. Flemming, former chairman of the United States Commission on Civil Rights, published its findings. In a report titled "Personal Justice Denied," the Commission stated that:

> The promulgation of Executive Order 9066 was not justified by military necessity and the decision which followed from it—detention, ending detention and ending exclusion—were not driven by analysis of military conditions. The broad historical causes which shaped these decisions were race prejudice, war hysteria, and a failure of political leadership. Widespread ignorance of Japanese Americans contributed to a policy conceived in haste and executed in an atmosphere of fear and anger at Japan. A grave injustice was done to American citizens and resident aliens of Japanese ancestry who, without individual review or any probative evidence against them, were excluded, removed, and detained by the United States during World War II.

The Commission therefore recommended that,

1.   on behalf of the United States, the President apologize to former evacuees for the injustices that had been perpetrated against them;

2. congress appropriate funds in order to support an educational program that would insure that the American public would be continually aware of the evacuation and the circumstances that lead to it; and

3. congress appropriate funds necessary to provide compensation of $20,000 for each surviving former evacuee.

On August 10, 1989, President Ronald Reagan signed the Civil Liberties Act of 1988, which implemented the recommendations of the Commission on Wartime Relocation and Internment of Civilians. Two years later, at a ceremony in Washington, D.C., the first $20,000 checks were presented to the oldest surviving former evacuees, along with a copy of a letter of apology signed by President George Bush.

◆   ◆   ◆

At the thirty-sixth biennial convention of the Japanese American Citizens League in Monterey, California, on July 1, 2000, a resolution was passed that recognized World War II Nisei draft resisters of conscience as principled Americans and offered an apology for the failure of the JACL to acknowledge the right of these men to refuse to be drafted until their constitutional rights had been restored. Although proponents took great pains to explain that the resolution was in no way intended to deemphasize the heroic sacrifices of the Nisei veterans who took a different course to regain the constitutional rights of Japanese Americans, the resolution was vehemently opposed by many veterans of World War II, who felt that the resolution amounted to a betrayal of former comrades-in-arms who had made the supreme sacrifice during World War II at the behest of the JACL.

0-595-29613-0

Printed in the United States
33953LVS00006B/195